NEW DIRECTIONS FOR COMMUNITY COLLEGES

Arthur M. Cohen
EDITOR-IN-CHIEF

Florence B. Brawer
ASSOCIATE EDITOR

Creating and Benefiting from Institutional Collaboration: Models for Success

Dennis McGrath
Community College of Philadelphia

EDITOR

Number 103, Fall 1998

JOSSEY-BASS PUBLISHERS
San Francisco

Clearinghouse for Community Colleges

CREATING AND BENEFITING FROM INSTITUTIONAL COLLABORATION:
MODELS FOR SUCCESS
Dennis McGrath (ed.)
New Directions for Community Colleges, no. 103
Volume XXVI, number 3
Arthur M. Cohen, Editor-in-Chief
Florence B. Brawer, Associate Editor

378.05
c9 v.2

New Directions for Community Colleges is indexed in Current Index to Journals in Education (ERIC).

Microfilm copies of issues and articles are available in 16mm and 35mm, as well as microfiche in 105mm, through University Microfilms Inc., 300 North Zeeb Road, Ann Arbor, Michigan 48106–1346.

ISSN 0194-3081   ISBN 0-7879-4236-7

NEW DIRECTIONS FOR COMMUNITY COLLEGES is part of The Jossey-Bass Higher and Adult Education Series and is published quarterly by Jossey-Bass Inc., Publishers, 350 Sansome Street, San Francisco, California 94104–1342, in association with the ERIC Clearinghouse for Community Colleges. Periodicals postage paid at San Francisco, California, and at additional mailing offices. POSTMASTER: Send address changes to New Directions for Community Colleges, Jossey-Bass Inc., Publishers, 350 Sansome Street, San Francisco, California 94104–1342.

SUBSCRIPTIONS cost $57.00 for individuals and $107.00 for institutions, agencies, and libraries. Prices subject to change.

THE MATERIAL in this publication is based on work sponsored wholly or in part by the Office of Educational Research and Improvement, U.S. Department of Education, under contract number RI-93-00-2003. Its contents do not necessarily reflect the views of the Department or any other agency of the U.S. Government.

EDITORIAL CORRESPONDENCE should be sent to the Editor-in-Chief, Arthur M. Cohen, at the ERIC Clearinghouse for Community Colleges, University of California, 3051 Moore Hall, 405 Hilgard Avenue, Los Angeles, California 90024–1521.

Cover photograph © Rene Sheret, After Image, Los Angeles, California, 1990.

www.josseybass.com

Printed in the United States of America on acid-free recycled paper containing 100 percent recovered waste paper, of which at least 20 percent is postconsumer waste.

CONTENTS

EDITOR'S NOTES

Community colleges are being reshaped by a variety of social, economic, and political forces that are creating new forms of cooperation and collective action among all types of organizations. In the corporate realm, business firms have dramatically changed from the nineteenth-century image of the autonomous, citadel-like organization. We now find many different organizational forms, especially ones involving long-term relationships with both suppliers and customers. To structure their dealings with one another, business firms are increasingly moving away from traditional, highly specific arm's length contracts toward much looser and open-ended contractual arrangements. These new business relationships range from informal links to arrangements so intricate that they begin to blur the boundaries between firms. Business analysts have identified a variety of new relationships, including joint ventures and consortia (Mariti and Smiley, 1983; Harrigan, 1985), strategic alliances (Gomes-Casseres, 1996), relational contracting (Goldberg, 1980), global coalitions (Porter and Fuller, 1986), networks (Powell, 1996), and coevolution and business ecosystems (Moore, 1996).

The political realm has seen dramatic change as well. The United States, Great Britain, and a number of European countries have shifted away from the interventionist national governments of the post–World War II era. This reduction in the role of the federal government is devolving responsibility to states and locales, accelerating the importance of local and regional alliances in promoting economic development. The vitality of communities increasingly depends on the capacity of local governments, businesses, and civic organizations to reach across traditional boundaries to leverage resources and maximize comparative advantage (Saxenian, 1994; Castells, 1996).

In the nonprofit world, we see the formation of a variety of service networks to address the challenges facing U.S. communities, and many organizations and agencies are developing new ways to coordinate and supply services. These include community-based consortia, public-private partnerships, for-profit joint ventures, and public-public cooperative efforts (Alter and Hage, 1993; Bailey and Koney, 1995; Harvey, 1993; Smale, 1993; Wallis, 1994).

In each case, organizations develop collaborative relationships because they see the benefits of working together. These arrangements add value to both for-profit and nonprofit operations and are increasingly critical to fulfilling core missions. Collaboration permits organizations to leverage scarce resources, reduce costs, link complementary competencies, and increase speed and flexibility.

Community colleges are also beginning to be shaped by this new organizational trend. Of course community colleges have long been involved with other institutions in their communities. They have sought out relationships with local school districts, business firms, social agencies, and community organizations as well as with other educational institutions. These relationships have fostered efforts such as customized job training, tech-prep courses, and transfer articulation agreements and also a variety of community service offerings. However, today we find many of our colleges involved in new and deeper forms of collaboration.

This volume offers a variety of examples of long-term, sophisticated, and influential collaborative efforts. Each began with external funding. However, in each case the institutional partners found ways to leverage their grant support to build durable, self-sustaining collaborative relationships. Consequently they can serve as useful models, even to institutions planning to draw on their own resources to launch collaborative efforts. Several of the chapter authors are part of the Ford Foundation's Urban Partnership Program, a sixteen-city collaborative educational reform effort to increase the number of underserved urban students receiving the baccalaureate degree. The other collaboratives described in this volume have received a mix of public and private support.

The new interinstitutional relationships are guided by a sense that central elements of the community college mission cannot be realized without sustained collaboration. For example, many community colleges are engaged in collaborative efforts to develop more effective ways to promote access and improve student achievement at every point along the educational pipeline.

Lindsay Wright and Rona Middleberg, in Chapter One, and Janet Lieberman, in Chapter Two, discuss the critical role community colleges can play as a nexus between high schools and four-year institutions. As Michael Gillespie demonstrates in Chapter Three, access and educational opportunity for at-risk students can be promoted in powerful ways through the development of neighborhood-based collaborations. Such collaborations recognize and build on the interdependencies that exist among community colleges and high schools, feeder middle and elementary schools, neighborhood social and health agencies, other community-based organizations, and parents. Héctor Garza and Ronald Eller, in Chapter Four, shift the focus from urban to rural areas, describing the role of rural community colleges in building collaboratives to promote economic development. These authors emphasize that in distressed rural communities, the most important role that community colleges can play is to foster relationships among local institutions in ways that link educational access and economic development.

As the contributors to this volume continually emphasize, collaboration must be understood both as a distinctive process and as a particular type of interorganizational structure. It differs most strikingly from other relationships, such as joint ventures, in its capacity to transform the participating organizations. Unlike more limited forms of cooperation, collaboration can deeply affect the internal structure, management style, identity, and mission of participating institutions as they learn to coordinate their collective resources.

Thus the process of collaboration poses special challenges and offers new opportunities that must be identified and carefully managed. Sara Lundquist and John Nixon, in Chapter Five, explore the new *partnership par-*

adigm and its implications for planning and management. Carolyn Williams, in Chapter Six, discusses ways of integrating collaboration into the leadership role of the community college president. Barbara Schaier-Peleg and Richard Donovan, in Chapter Seven, describe the role of a managing partner in promoting foundation-funded collaborations and emphasize the vital role community colleges can play in promoting interorganizational relationships. L. Steven Zwerling complements this analysis by offering a funder's perspective on collaboratives in Chapter Eight. In Chapter Nine, Laura Rendón, Wendy Gans, and Mistalene Calleroz discuss the essential role of assessment in advancing collaboration. They provide a detailed picture of the many issues that must be addressed by the various institutional stakeholders so that assessment can guide decision making and program development. Finally, in Chapter Ten, Erika Yamasaki describes a number of resources that those undertaking collaborative partnerships may find useful.

In sum, this volume explores the challenges and opportunities that collaboration presents for community colleges. Because we are just beginning to fully understand the many ways in which collaboration both benefits and affects the participating organizations, the contributing authors emphasize practical examples and lessons learned as well as practices and models that can be used by a variety of institutions. At the outset we can consider the following lessons, derived from reflection on the best of contemporary collaborative efforts:

Collaboration often produces flatter organizations with fuzzy boundaries. This result can increase flexibility in our colleges but requires new styles of management to promote the transition. Lundquist and Nixon illustrate these issues by analyzing how one community college realigned its administrative structure to promote a more collaborative culture.

Collaboration emphasizes that community problems are interconnected. The process of collaboration encourages communication among a variety of institutions, which can stimulate new, joint approaches to solving problems. This is reflected in a number of innovative programs that encourage joint problem definition and problem solving among partners. Examples include the corridor initiative described by Gillespie, the Extending Transfer and Middle College programs discussed by Lieberman, and the Summer Scholars Transfer Institute reported by Lundquist and Nixon. Garza and Eller review how a collaborative approach helps community colleges promote rural development by identifying the interconnections among education, social services, and economic development.

Collaboration builds relationships even among institutions that are ostensibly competitors. As boundaries become blurred through joint efforts, new and more complex organizational networks are formed. For example, the Corridor Initiative and Middle College programs establish links between community colleges and school systems, and Extending Transfer builds relationships between community colleges and four-year institutions.

Collaborations promote new relationships with funders. As grantmakers turn to collaboratives to increase the impact of funded initiatives, new relationships are developing between community colleges and their funders. Zwerling describes this new relationship from the perspective of the funder, and Schaier-Peleg and Donovan analyze the role of a managing partner in a privately funded initiative.

Successful collaboration requires a commitment to assessment. As Rendón, Gans, and Calleroz illustrate, interinstitutional relationships call for new forms of participatory assessment to guide planning and action.

Dennis McGrath
Editor

References

Alter, C., and Hage, J. *Organizations Working Together.* Thousand Oaks, Calif.: Sage, 1993.

Bailey, D., and Koney, K. "An Integrative Framework for the Evaluation of Community-Based Consortia." *Evaluation and Program Planning,* 1995, *18* (3); 245–252.

Castells, M. *The Rise of the Network Society.* Vol. 1. Cambridge, Mass.: Blackwell, 1996.

Goldberg, V. "Relational Exchange: Economics and Complex Contracts." *American Behavioral Scientist,* 1980, *23,* 337–352.

Gomes-Casseres, B. *The Alliance Revolution: The New Shape of Business Rivalry.* Cambridge, Mass.: Harvard University Press, 1996.

Harrigan, K. *Strategies for Joint Ventures.* Lexington, Mass.: Heath, 1985.

Harvey, L. "Public-Private Nonprofit Partnerships for Breaking Welfare Dependency." *National Civic Review,* Winter 1993, pp. 16–24.

Mariti, P., and Smiley, R. "Co-Operative Agreements and the Organization of Industry." *Journal of Industrial Economics,* 1983, *31,* 437–451.

Moore, J. F. *The Death of Competition.* New York: Harper Business, 1996.

Porter, M., and Fuller, M. "Coalitions and Global Strategy." In M. Porter (ed.), *Competition in Global Industries.* Boston: Harvard Business School Press, 1986.

Powell, W. W. "Neither Market nor Hierarchy: Network Forms of Organization." In G. Thompson (ed.), *Markets, Hierarchies, and Networks: The Coordination of Social Life.* Thousand Oaks, Calif.: Sage, 1996.

Saxenian, A. *Regional Advantage.* Cambridge, Mass.: Harvard University Press, 1994.

Smale, G. "The Nature of Innovation and Community-Based Practice." In E. Martinez-Brawley and S. Delvan (eds.), *Transferring Technology in the Personal Social Services.* Silver Springs, Md.: NASW Books, 1993.

Wallis, A. *Networks: Trust and Values.* Denver: National Civic League Press, 1994.

DENNIS MCGRATH is professor of sociology at the Community College of Philadelphia and senior fellow for assessment at the National Center for Urban Partnerships.

A collaboration between the NYU School of Education and eleven area community colleges encourages community college students to transfer and to pursue teaching and human service careers.

Lessons from a Long-Term Collaboration

Lindsay M. Wright, Rona Middleberg

The New York University (NYU) School of Education is a professional school whose mission is to prepare students for a wide range of careers in the human services. In the late 1980s, under the leadership of Dean Ann Marcus, the school began to focus its energies on urban needs and set out to establish a range of programs that would take into account the diverse racial and ethnic populations of the nation's cities. This involved recruiting students from underserved populations and encouraging them to commit themselves to serving urban areas after graduation. Because community colleges serve as the entry point into higher education for a majority of minority and low-income students, the school set out to create a program that would reach out to academically qualified community college students to help them transfer and complete their baccalaureate degrees at the NYU School of Education.

Prior to 1989, only fifteen to twenty community college students annually transferred to the School of Education. Attempting to significantly increase the number of student transfers, the Community College Transfer Opportunity Program (CCTOP) was developed. It is a collaboration between the NYU School of Education and eleven tri-state community colleges: Bergen Community College, Borough of Manhattan Community College, Bronx Community College, Housatonic Community-Technical College, Kingsborough Community College, La Guardia Community College, Middlesex County College, Nassau Community College, Queensborough Community College, Rockland Community College, and Westchester Community College. During the past eight years, the collaborative has enabled more than 550 community college students (45 percent of them African American or Hispanic) to transfer to NYU to complete baccalaureate degrees in education, nursing, applied psychology, communication studies, nutrition, music, dance, and art.

The program has three components: it aims to facilitate the transfer process and enhance student retention by using articulation agreements that minimize credit loss, by offering scholarship assistance to help overcome financial need, and by providing a centralized source of information and guidance to students from the time of their community college studies, through their transition to NYU, and until they graduate from the university.

A Brief History

Although a number of articulation agreements were in place prior to the collaborative, the School of Education had few community college transfer students. Prospective transfer students faced a myriad of obstacles, among them the high cost of tuition, the loss of transfer credits, the difficulties of negotiating the complex administrative structure of the university, and the general perception that NYU was not community college transfer student friendly. After extensive discussions with community college presidents, academic deans, transfer counselors, and students, it became clear to CCTOP's founding codirectors, Martin Moed and Lindsay Wright, that if we in the School of Education were serious about increasing the number of community college students who transferred, we needed to work more collaboratively with the community colleges to create a comprehensive program that would not only provide access but actively encourage it.

We initially approached community colleges chosen with an eye toward a diverse student population, geographic proximity, and academic program offerings of high quality. After gaining the support of the college presidents, we proceeded to learn more about the colleges' academic programs and discovered that before we could write effective transfer agreements, our school's academic requirements would need to be somewhat modified. During the first year, the School of Education adjusted liberal arts requirements for eighteen of its baccalaureate programs, and we drafted nearly 180 transfer agreements. These agreements indicated how credits would transfer and which courses would remain to be completed at NYU.

The articulation documents were intended to be both advisory and contractual instruments, designed to make it easier for community college students to plan a course of study and to transfer with confidence. It also enabled the NYU admissions office to provide students with faster and more consistent information about their transfer credits, because most courses no longer had to be reviewed by the faculty but were preapproved by the agreements.

This work formed the basis for dialogue between NYU faculty and their counterparts at the community colleges. Throughout the initial planning year, meetings were held to draft the agreements, learn about each other's programs, and establish new collegial relationships.

In order to address the financial obstacle facing most of the prospective transfer students, the School of Education has earmarked scholarship funds to be awarded to students transferring from the CCTOP consortium colleges. The

Community College Transfer Opportunity Program Scholarship has been established, and each year administrators, faculty, and transfer counselors at the community colleges are invited to nominate qualified students. This nomination process has proven an excellent mechanism for publicizing the program, increasing the involvement of community college faculty and counselors in the transfer function, and creating natural opportunities for communication between NYU and the community colleges.

Last, we established the CCTOP Office, which is dedicated to helping community college students, faculty, and transfer counselors negotiate NYU's large, complex administrative structure. The CCTOP director provides a centralized source of information and guidance and serves as a liaison between the community colleges and the various offices and departments at the university. Emphasis is on creating a friendly, responsive atmosphere so that CCTOP is not only about access in theory but also about community college students and personnel actually experiencing NYU as accessible.

CCTOP's services do not end once a student enrolls at the university. Although all students are mainstreamed (there are no special courses or support programs per se), CCTOP continues to serves as a touchstone, a familiar place students can come when they have a problem, need assistance in negotiating the university, or want a sounding board for their experiences.

The CCTOP model has been successful by many measures. Since 1990, as mentioned earlier, more than 550 students have transferred through CCTOP, 45 percent of them students of color. Enrollments have increased consistently, from 23 students in 1990–91 to 112 in 1997–98. Our overall retention rate for full-time students is 86 percent, with the majority of students who leave doing so for financial or personal, not academic, reasons. Two hundred and sixty students have already graduated, 26 percent of them with honors. Twenty-five students are currently enrolled in graduate programs; eighteen have already earned their master's degrees.

Barriers to Successful Collaboration

In establishing CCTOP, we faced both structural and cultural obstacles. Structural barriers included the perception that it would be difficult if not impossible to attain a close fit between a private four-year university and urban community colleges: Could courses be considered to be equivalent? How could the dramatic differences in tuition and fees be bridged? Would university faculty be willing to work collaboratively with community college faculty? Among the cultural or environmental obstacles were concerns about students' belief in their ability to succeed in an academically challenging environment and their self-doubts about fitting in at an elite private university. Less discussed were faculty issues—the doubts that community college faculty might have about their students and their own institution's ability to produce academically capable students. In the early days of CCTOP, it was not uncommon for us to be asked, "Why would NYU want to recruit our students?" and,

"Where were you when *we* were trying to initiate articulation agreements?" Some community college faculty objected to our efforts, protesting that we were going to skim the cream of the best students out of the public system. We certainly wanted to encourage transfer, but we were also concerned about appearing to guarantee to participating faculty and students that the arrangement would work.

Lessons Learned

Drawing from the program's first eight years of history, we have gathered lessons that may be of value to institutions seeking to establish programs similar to CCTOP.

Do your homework. If program leaders are to design a transfer program that not only meets the needs of particular students but also works well with the different organizational structure and culture of each community college, it is important that they spend considerable time visiting community college campuses and meeting with transfer counselors, advisers, administrators, and students.

For example, CCTOP directors visited four campuses, spoke with various administrators and faculty, and met with small groups of students. They learned how many students transferred each year, which colleges they attended and why (cost, location, ease of transfer, parental advice), and what they chose to study; how faculty, administrators, and students perceived NYU; the major barriers to transfer that students encountered at NYU and other private institutions; which faculty and administrative offices advised students about transfer; and how important transfer was to the mission of each community college.

Create the framework. It is imperative that you distill the information gathered from talking to members of the community college faculty, staff, and student body to determine the key factors you must address in order to have a successful program. These factors should be identified early because they will guide the direction of subsequent activities. For example, after meeting with community college deans, administrators, transfer counselors, and students, the CCTOP directors discerned that three issues needed to be addressed in order to have a successful program: the loss of transfer credits, the cost of attending a private university, and the administrative and psychological barriers impeding transfer. In response CCTOP created flexible articulation agreements that guaranteed the transfer of at least sixty credits, an exclusive scholarship fund for prospective students from partner colleges, and an adviser to provide support to both transfer counselors and prospective students.

Get support from the top and build down. For collaborations to work well, it is crucial that the head of the four-year institution reach out directly to community college presidents and get their support for the initiative and their commitment to its success. For example, the dean of the NYU School of Education personally invited the presidents of nine targeted community colleges to join the CCTOP consortium and to work with the School of Education as full partners in the design and promotion of CCTOP on their campuses and in the recruitment of their students. We discussed their students' needs and asked for their expertise.

Identify a top academic official at each community college to serve as liaison to the transfer program. The active involvement of academic deans or vice presidents is important for practical and symbolic reasons. Their participation reinforces the idea that promoting transfer is a valued and important academic goal of the institution. Because they provide direct access to the faculty, they also facilitate much of the work of building a transfer program. Their liaison responsibilities should be well defined. For example, the dean of the NYU School of Education hosted a luncheon for CCTOP's academic liaisons specifically to discuss issues of transfer and to get their recommendations for building a transfer program in partnership with them. These liaisons were asked to arrange opportunities for CCTOP staff to meet with department chairs to discuss the transfer program, and to facilitate the review and approval of articulation agreements. In return, CCTOP promised to provide data on their students and to keep them informed of the program's progress.

Involve the liaisons and transfer counselors in the program's implementation phase. When program directors provide opportunities for faculty and administrators to have a voice in the development of the transfer program and actively solicit their advice, the program will become more responsive to the needs of the community colleges and their students and will be more flexible and open to new ideas and change. For example, CCTOP directors worked closely with community college transfer counselors in the development of new articulation agreements. The counselors reviewed drafts, suggested different formats, recommended ways to clarify language, and helped identify the kinds of things that good transfer agreements should communicate to students. We threw out initial agreements and created new versions when transfer counselors responded negatively to our first attempts. We sent drafts of agreements to our academic liaisons for their comments and suggestions, and we asked them to send the final agreements to their department chairs for review and signature.

Don't neglect your own faculty. A good transfer program requires the commitment of the faculty at the four-year institution. To ensure effective transfer agreements, faculty must be willing to acknowledge the academic legitimacy of community college coursework. This often requires reeducating faculty about community colleges, their missions, and their students. For example, we gathered historical data on students who had previously transferred from community colleges, and analyzed their incoming and graduating grade point averages and their graduation rates. We met with each undergraduate program director in our school to discuss his or her perceptions of community college students, shared our data, and reviewed our plans. We addressed directly prejudices and misconceptions about community college preparation and stressed our dean's commitment to diversity and to serving urban populations. Most faculty were receptive to the program and supported it. Others were more resistant to our recruitment plans, and we spent many hours talking about their concerns, which ranged from thinly veiled racism to fears that community college students would be poorly prepared for advanced undergraduate coursework. Some of these faculty "joined" CCTOP only in its third year of operation, when it became clear that CCTOP was attracting large numbers of academically qualified students.

Develop and implement a comprehensive marketing strategy. Think broadly and creatively about the many different ways to get the word out about your new program. Develop strategies for targeting desirable graduates. Understand the image others have of your institution, and address that image directly in your marketing strategies. Monitor your results, discarding those efforts that elicit few responses and expanding those that elicit many. For example, CCTOP does the following:

Involves the community college academic deans, transfer counselors, and faculty by asking them to nominate students for CCTOP scholarships

Publishes an individualized brochure for each participating community college; distributes the brochures at community college transfer fairs; and sends them to faculty, transfer counselors, and students

Works with community college public relations directors to place stories in the local press

Promotes the transfer program in community college and NYU bulletins and other official publications

Produces posters to hang on community college bulletin boards

Places ads in student newspapers

Maintains a mailing list of faculty and sends personalized letters about the program, asking faculty for their support

Invites community college students to open houses, information sessions, and transfer days at NYU

Develop a communications strategy for preserving and strengthening your collaborative. Consistent and frequent verbal and written communication with presidents, academic liaisons, transfer counselors, faculty, and students will ensure smooth operations, build trust and support, and provide ongoing feedback about the program's progress. Personal letters, notes, and telephone calls help reinforce the sense of ownership among your community college partners and encourage them to publicize your efforts more broadly, thereby helping you to attract and recruit the kinds of students who will transfer to your school. For example, we have established a regular flow of communication to different people at our partner colleges:

Presidents and academic liaisons receive an annual report in the fall that includes a list of students from their college who enrolled through CCTOP and also those who graduated during the previous year.

Transfer counselors receive numerous mailings including the annual report, updates on academic programs and scholarship opportunities, and copies of newsletters and news articles featuring CCTOP students. They also gather at NYU for an annual transfer counselor luncheon, which gives them the opportunity to talk with each other about transfer issues and to try out new ideas.

Faculty receive updates on the students they have nominated, a personal thank-you letter from the dean, and an annual letter reminding them about the program and their important role in advising students about transfer and nominating them for CCTOP scholarships. Some NYU School of Education department chairs also write directly to community college faculty about their specific baccalaureate degree programs.

Students receive personalized responses to their inquiries, letters confirming their nominations, scholarship award letters, and other correspondence during the admissions process.

Building on CCTOP

In addition to its core mission of improving access, CCTOP has provided an infrastructure that has enabled us to broaden and deepen our involvement with community colleges and has enabled the CCTOP community colleges to become more engaged with both the School of Education and the university at large. For example, working with many of the CCTOP community college presidents, the school has created the Center for Urban Community College Leadership, which offers a doctoral program and also seminars and institutes focused on issues particularly relevant to urban community colleges. Four of the CCTOP community college presidents serve on the center's national board of visitors. The director of the center, Joshua Smith, is a former community college president and a former chancellor of the California community college system. In another instance, the NYU Division of Nursing and the Borough of Manhattan Community College Department of Nursing worked together to explore and develop alternative teaching strategies, including ways to integrate multimedia technology into academic curricula. As a third example, faculty at the CCTOP community colleges are invited to participate in the university's prestigious Faculty Resource Network, a consortium of twenty-seven liberal arts institutions linked with NYU for the purpose of faculty development.

Conclusion

The Community College Transfer Opportunity Program provides advantages to the students who participate, the faculties of all the colleges including New York University, and the institutions themselves.

Students. Clearly the rate at which CCTOP students graduate from NYU, the primary indicator of success, is a major benefit for those students. Often not discussed, however, are the significant financial benefits to the students. Not only do they receive scholarships and thereby see their NYU tuition bill lowered, but the relationship between NYU and the feeder community colleges allows students to earn an NYU degree at about half the cost they would incur if they began attending NYU as freshmen. Although there are significant intrinsic advantages to attending NYU for four rather than two years, for students from low-income backgrounds, the CCTOP structure offers a fine alternative.

Faculties. They too win—and on both sides of the CCTOP equation. First, the NYU faculty benefit by having a more diverse and excellent student body. Eight years of data show that CCTOP students not only graduate on time but at high levels of achievement. Disproportionate numbers of CCTOP students receive Latin honors, serve in elected and leadership positions, and go on to graduate school. The faculty at NYU, who prior to CCTOP were in many cases skeptical about the ability of community college students to thrive in NYU's academic environment, find their attitudes challenged and ultimately changed. This makes it easier for subsequent cohorts of two-year college students, because educators' expectations about students' academic potential have a dramatic impact on how students fare.

The community college faculty benefit as well. They too, in many cases, have had attitudes about the potential of their students that needed examination. Studies have shown that too many do not believe that their students have the capacity to excel in challenging academic environments. In the words of Richardson, Fisk, and Okun (1983) they *level down* their academic demands to fit their view of the two-year college students' limited academic ability. Now, the gathering evidence from the success of CCTOP students at NYU has begun to cause faculty at participating community colleges to take another look at their students, and not just those they nominate to CCTOP.

Institutions. Finally, all institutions have benefited from a more diverse student body and elevated expectations. Among all those who have worked together through the years on its development and implementation, the CCTOP partnership has contributed to a sense of optimism about what can be accomplished through collaboration.

Reference

Richardson, R. C., Jr., Fisk, E. C., and Okun, M. A. *Literacy in the Open-Access College.* San Francisco: Jossey-Bass, 1983.

LINDSAY M. WRIGHT *is assistant dean for planning at the New York University School of Education and one of the founders of the Community College Transfer Opportunity Program.*

RONA MIDDLEBERG *is director of the Community College Transfer Opportunity Program at the New York University School of Education.*

Two innovative programs to reduce attrition and promote student achievement, Middle College and Exploring Transfer, exemplify the best practices involved in community college collaborations with high schools and four-year institutions.

Creating Structural Change: Best Practices

Janet E. Lieberman

The story of the community college movement is a tale of rapid expansion, multiple agendas, and diverse missions. Initiated as an institution to provide access, to offer transfer as well as terminal education, and to initiate lifelong learning opportunities, the two-year college now confronts an identity crisis. Time has created a disconnect between the original missions and current reality. The mission of the two-year college needs reappraisal for the next century, but one function remains essential. According to Arthur Cohen and Florence Brawer, the American community college "was founded to serve as a link between the lower schools and establishments of higher learning" (Cohen and Brawer, 1987, p. xi). That commitment was a cornerstone of La Guardia Community College when it was established in 1971.

History

As the newest unit in the higher education system of the City University of New York, La Guardia was expected to develop innovative solutions to urban education problems. At that time, at least 40 percent of the pupils in New York failed to complete high school; of those who did graduate high school, about one out of four went to college. Clearly, this degree of attrition reduced the admission rate to the two-year institutions. In response, the university vice chancellor directed La Guardia "to do something about keeping adolescents in high school and attracting them to college." The president of La Guardia assigned me, his special assistant, to develop an institutional response. I spent two years analyzing and researching the problem and then securing funding for an innovative model that would meet the educational challenge. The prevailing idea was a collaboration between high school and college, to be called Middle College.

Principles of Planning

Planning for collaboration requires a hard look at what is and an optimistic outlook at what could be. Developing innovative structures demands knowing the designs that work, analyzing the practices that fail, and comprehending how to redesign the model. To solve the problem of reducing the drop-out rate and encouraging more students to attend college, the La Guardia staff first spent two years studying the school-college connections existing nationally. The research showed that

The highest proportion of drop-outs in urban schools occurs in the ninth and tenth grades.

Dropping out is not a function of students' inability to master the academic content but a function of school structural anomalies: anonymity, bureaucracy, and irrelevancy. A better solution would be a student-centered program.

Developmental psychology principles suggested that a fifteen-year-old has more in common with an eighteen-year-old than with a twelve-year-old. That reality-based observation argued for a high school–college collaborative as a way of advancing the seamless web of schooling.

Successful models in private educational settings proved the feasibility of combining high school and the initial years of college education.

Any national model fostering collaboration between two levels of the educational system has to involve both those levels in its planning. The two years of developmental activity for our program (from 1972 to 1974) required many meetings with secondary and higher education officials at the state, city, and borough levels. A meeting at Albany, the state capital, to present the Middle College concept was the first time in state history that the higher education and the secondary systems sat together at a planning table. Planning outside La Guardia Community College called for patience, diplomacy, and fortitude. Planning inside the college to convince faculty and staff of the idea's value took negotiation, manipulation, and a dual appeal to monetary rewards and moral integrity. Key to planning in any collaborative is strong leadership at the top and voluntarism in the rank and file, and we had both in designing and implementing Middle College.

Description of the Model

The design that evolved still remains intact at La Guardia and in the thirty-one replications nationwide. Middle College, the first public high school–college collaboration in the country, aims at attracting potential drop-outs and high-risk students. It is an alternative high school established jointly by the New York City Board of Education and the New York Board of Higher Education. The school's five hundred students are urban disadvantaged underachievers, with black and Hispanic groups representing more than half of the school population. They come voluntarily from local schools at the end of the eighth grade, and enter a combined high school–college program on the college site. Here, they share facilities with college students, and have the opportunity to take college classes. The program includes ninth through twelfth grade, but depending on ability and on motivation, the students progress at their own rate. Middle College has a twenty-two-year history and some remarkable success stories.

Today, Middle Colleges throughout the country report a student retention rate of 85 percent; 75 percent of seniors graduate, and 78 percent of that portion go on to college. La Guardia now supports and sustains two additional alternative high schools on its campus: International High School, addressed to Limited English Proficient students, and the institute for Arts and Technology, a program dedicated to high-risk students who have an interest in media and technology. The Middle School collaborative received an Outstanding Innovation in American Government award in 1997, one of twenty-five programs cited in a competition of 1,500 institutions.

The collaboration benefits both the high school and the college in a myriad of ways.

It increases the pool of students going to college.

It enables college faculty to influence high school curriculum and content mastery.

It allows faculty at both sites to share a realistic knowledge of expectations and achievement levels of incoming students.

It allows high school students to take college courses, reducing the total time they spend in school and increasing motivation.

It gives the college an enhanced reputation in the community as an institution serving the public. This results in greater enrollment for continuing education programs and more freshmen coming to La Guardia.

It allows both the high school and the college to apply for a broader range of federal and state grants.

The planning and the teaching in Middle College reflect the practices of La Guardia: full participation in cooperative education, broad interdisciplinary learning, and wide use of learning communities. Part of the planning called for a reassignment of mandatory faculty positions, with a higher proportion of guidance counselors but the same overall budgetary allocation as other New York City high schools. The school is small, five hundred students maximum, but the size is not the only critical factor in its success. It is a holistic model, designed after we looked at the problems of the student in a regular school and developed an institution that would

- Raise aspirations
- Enrich the setting
- Reduce fear and anonymity
- Replace failure with success
- Provide a sense of the future

The trick is to embody these abstractions in a practice teaching and learning institution that runs on tax levy money. Any model that depends on soft money is doomed, because the soft money usually disappears after three years, and administrators cannot plan long term without the assurance of continued funding. Similarly, innovative models are most successful when all participants—students, teachers, and administrators—sign on voluntarily. Choice and options, embodied in voluntarism, give people in collaboratives a sense of working together to reach a goal.

A Corollary Model

About ten years after founding Middle College, La Guardia met the challenge of the upper half of the collaborative sequence: joining the two-year college to a four-year institution. In this instance, the Ford Foundation stimulated the effort, through the Transfer Opportunities Program. La Guardia was invited to respond to the program RFP, and Exploring Transfer, a partnership between La Guardia and Vassar College, emerged (Lieberman and Hunger, 1997). The role of the community college was critical to the collaboration. La Guardia initiated the ideas, worked out the partnerships, hosted the meetings, supplied planners and consultant faculty, and in some cases administered the planning funds.

Description. Exploring Transfer is a collaboration between seven community colleges and Vassar College that allows two-year students to spend five weeks on the Vassar campus in a mini college program. They take two academic courses, pitched at the Vassar level of intensity and requirements, attend a required writing lab, and earn seven academic credits. They live in the dorms, on a rural campus seventy-five miles north of New York City. All courses are team taught by one community college faculty member and one four-year faculty member. All participants volunteer. The program has a twelve-year history; there has been one drop-out in that time, and 64 percent of the five hundred participants have acquired a B.A. degree, three times the national average of successful transfers.

Principles of Planning. The principles of planning were similar to those embodied in launching Middle College: that is, looking at the student, examining instruction, improving the process. As in the high school collaboration, leadership at the top of both institutions was essential: presidents had to signal their approval and initially clear the way for faculty to plan. In Exploring Transfer, after the initial institutional commitment, faculty from both schools ran the program, determined the criteria for admission, and generally assumed responsibility for the program. The key component responsible for the success of the program has been mutual trust between the two-year and four-year personnel. Trust is a much talked about but seldomly integrated principle in collaborative endeavors, yet it is the sine qua non for success. Unfortunately there is little trust between levels of education; instead there has more typically been mutual blame. Developing a sense of shared mission takes time and requires dedication to a student-centered approach.

Exploring Transfer, like Middle College, removes the obstacles to achievement and enables students to use their minds and develop their abilities. These opportunities to uncover their hidden hopes and stretch academically promote students' self-esteem and increase their success. The Vassar campus setting eliminates the usual distractions of families, jobs, and multiple responsibilities and permits the luxury of full-time study. However, at both Middle College, located at the community college, and Exploring Transfer, held at a four-year, ivy league, liberal arts college. developing an enriched learning environment that substitutes security for fear, encouragement for disappointment, and successful peers for discouraged classmates creates programs where there are no losers.

The Lessons of Success

The successes of both Exploring Transfer and Middle College suggest the following deep revisions in practices that surround contemporary collaboration:

Voluntarism is the key to success: all participants—students, faculty, and staff—have to elect to be involved.

All innovative collaborations need to concentrate on the student. Why don't students currently succeed? What are the institutional factors that create students' negative attitudes, fears, and inability to display their potential?

Successful collaboratives attest to the power of maximizing learning through students' studying together in groups. The campus environment that fosters learning communities enriches learning.

Team teaching, with faculty from different levels of schooling, creates valuable examples of dialogue and divergent opinions that enrich both students and teachers. Each teacher who participates in cross-level instruction brings valuable insights back to colleagues; the ripple effect begins to promote the seamless web.

As those involved observe and define common ground in helping students make academic connections between one level of learning and the next, a body of pedagogical practices in transition learning and teaching is emerging. Eventually, a body of knowledge incorporating these practices will have the potential to supplant remediation.

When there is initially strong leadership from the top administrative level, faculty, given time and decision-making power, can run collaborative programs.

Finally, a range of unexpected outcomes derives from collaborations. One of the most important outcomes is the energizing and renewal of faculty, who respond creatively to new challenges and find great stimulation in solving the academic problems presented. Team teaching is invigorating and regenerates interest in content areas. Combining different levels of education opens horizons not only for faculty but also for students and administrators. Other institutions have come to recognize the academic talents of some nontraditional students, as is exemplified in adaptations of Exploring Transfer at Bucknell University and Smith College.

A program like Exploring Transfer has the potential to address the problems of inequity and lack of access in a relatively simple way. The transforming force of intensive Liberal Arts study in a residential college program suggests a partial solution to broadening the pool of students available for a baccalaureate degree. It also reinforces the mission of the public community college to offer opportunities for nontraditional students, for those who otherwise would not have access to a college education. That mission needs reinforcement today more than ever, and collaboratives are the key to keeping it alive. When educators enable students to finish high school and move into college, as they do in the Middle College structure, the college-going rate increases. La Guardia has a twenty-two-year experience with data proving the increase. Moreover, most of the thirty-one replications document the same degree of improvement. Whereas the number of urban high school students who graduate runs about one out of four, or about 25 percent, in many inner-city populations, Middle Colleges generally show three times that rate, with 75 percent of their freshman classes graduating high school. The same phenomenon occurs in the role that the community college plays in the Exploring Transfer program. The rate of student transfers from two- to four-year institutions is almost three times the national average. The program has a 64 percent transfer rate, whereas the national average is 23 percent.

Why is this important now? What has ensuring the continuity of education and increasing the pool of two-year students who achieve the baccalaureate degree to do with the future of two-year institutions? Most of the answers lie in defining the appropriate role of the community college. Currently the dialogue about that role centers around restoring the collegiate function of the community college, but the societal implications of this dialogue are extremely broad. Educational collaboratives play a positive role in maximizing that collegiate function.

In large cities, the future of the community college is threatened. Whether this is a reaction to the increasing national conservatism or the result of a pointed attack on the underprivileged, the educational consequence is an emphasis on state testing, increased standards, and limited access. Add to this the loss of affirmative action, and the result is a predetermined decrease in opportunities for what Patricia Cross (1971) called the *new student,* the backbone of the two-year enrollment. Most two-year institutions have reacted by becoming brokers between business and education (vocational courses), between failures of the system and substitute accreditation (GED courses), and between immigrants and the mainstream college (ESL courses).

The continuing education function of the community college has gone from school cash cow to school life support system, but these activities are usually short term, dependent on outside funding or student payment, not oriented toward the liberal arts, and lacking in opportunities for further education. Simultaneously, the remedial function of the degree-granting division of the two-year institution is under severe threat. It is important to look at this trend in the light of the past and the future role of the community college.

In fact, an interesting paradox exists. Although the trend is to restrict opportunities for the average two-year student, there are increasing calls for broad student preparation to help the United States participate in the global economy. It is time to ask some questions:

If the community college lacks the resources to educate the nontraditional student, who will pick up the challenge?

If access and equity are denied and affirmative action is nullified, how will deserving minority students acquire the education necessary to participate in a democracy and to gain future employment in a global economy?

If the two-year college loses the opportunity to serve its constituency and its community, what will be the costs to cities in crime, violence, and unemployment?

How can we motivate and provide social mobility for the new immigrant student without the promise and rewards of college education?

And finally, in its own self-interest, doesn't higher education require the diversity of the transfer student to promote vitality and dialogue in the classroom?

Collaboratives across the artificial educational divides are not the only answer, but they are the best, the easiest, and the cheapest. School-college partnerships and two- to four-year collaboratives have a very successful track record in two significant areas: enhancing motivation and increasing the number of baccalaureate degree students. Both outcomes address the promise of U.S. democracy and the problem of economic development. Therein lies the future of the community college.

References

Cohen, A., and Brawer, F. *The Collegiate Function of Community Colleges.* San Francisco: Jossey-Bass, 1987.

Cross, K. P. *Beyond the Open Door: New Students to Higher Education.* San Francisco: Jossey-Bass, 1971.

Lieberman, J., and Hunger, J. Y. *Transforming Students' Lives: How "Exploring Transfer" Works, and Why.* Washington, D.C.: American Association for Higher Education, 1997.

JANET E. LIEBERMAN is special assistant to the president at La Guardia Community College.

The Bronx Corridor of Success is a collaborative attempt to promote systemic educational reform in a low-income community. It links schools across all educational sectors with health institutions, social agencies, community organizations, and parents.

An Urban Intervention That Works: The Bronx Corridor of Success

Michael C. Gillespie

It was Carl Polowczyk, the former dean of Bronx Community College, a passionate visionary for all seasons, who coined the phrase that most captures the purpose of the Bronx Corridor of Success Initiative. Having worked in the south central Bronx for thirty-seven years, Carl had witnessed the downward spiral of poverty, crime, and joblessness that characterized the neighborhoods surrounding the campus. He believed that the Corridor of Success could vastly improve the quality of life for children, youths, and families in the neighborhood most immediate to the college. Once that neighborhood, the University Heights–Tremont section, was restored, the corridor initiative could then be replicated throughout the various other communities of the borough. In this way, as Carl so aptly put it, the corridor ultimately could "take back the Bronx one neighborhood at a time."

Vision

The Bronx Corridor of Success Initiative involves a select group of feeder schools serving kindergarten through college students in the south central Bronx. It represents a systematic collaboration of educational, social, and community organizations, institutions that enhance the academic preparation, social attainment, health, and quality of life of children, youths, and families in the borough.

The corridor initiative began in 1992 with funding from the Ford Foundation. At that time, Bronx Community College planned to create a model middle school on campus that could serve as a professional development or laboratory school for educators and students in the surrounding community.

The Ford funding enabled the college to secure an additional five-year grant from the Danforth Foundation for additional strategic planning. However, my team and I could not obtain sufficient monies from the New York City Board of Education to renovate the college building chosen for the middle school site. Therefore the college decided to forego creating the model middle school and instead began to develop school-college collaboratives—first by working solely with Intermediate School 82 (from 1993 to 1994) and then expanding to all levels—elementary, middle, and high school and college (from 1994 to the present).

Responding to the Community

The University Heights–Tremont section of the south central Bronx is located in the poorest congressional district in the United States. This neighborhood is marked by high rates of drug abuse, teen pregnancy, AIDS, crime, unemployment, and adult illiteracy. The population increasingly consists of immigrant, transient, and single-parent households, with over 85 percent of these households below the poverty level. These factors contribute to chronic educational failure—poor attendance, low academic achievement, and high dropout rates—at every educational level. Many students enter school lacking basic skills in reading, writing, and mathematics and are therefore poorly prepared to meet the challenges of high school, let alone college or the world of work and careers.

To respond to these problems, the corridor initiative took a collaborative, holistic approach, creating a network among the public education institutions in the community that serve elementary through college students. Each of these schools contains a population that is at least 96 percent minority, with over 62 percent Hispanic and limited English proficient students. The vast majority of students in all of the corridor schools live below the poverty level.

These schools already enjoyed an established feeder pattern within Community School District 9 and the Bronx High School Division, as follows: the two elementary schools, P.S. 104 and P.S. 204 (grades K–5), feed into Intermediate School 82 (grades 6–8); P.S. 109 (grades K–4) students can go on to I.S. 82 after they complete grade 5 at another school; I.S. 82 then feeds into Roosevelt High School and Taft High School (grades 9–12). Large numbers of graduates of these two high schools later attend Bronx Community College, and a high percentage of these students then attend Lehman College for bachelor's degrees.

My team and I began by drawing on the informal relationships that already existed in this network. We then invited additional local organizations to serve as partners to the schools to address social and health needs of corridor constituencies. These organizations included the Morris Heights Health Center, St. Barnabas Hospital, and Pius XII Family Services, a local community-based social services organization. All these schools and groups were brought together to form the Corridor of Success Steering Committee, which thus included parents and educators representing all grade levels from kindergarten through college and municipal, health care, social service, and business professionals. The corridor steering committee provided a forum for discussion, and the group ultimately defined a number of goals for the initiative:

Educational goals for students and faculty included decreases in drop-out rates and increases in student attendance, in students taking advanced courses, in on-time graduation rates, and in students performing at or above grade level.

Health goals for students, families, and the community included increases in immunizations for students and their families; increased access to health, dental, psychological, and social services; and decreases in substance abuse and serious illness in the community.

Socioeconomic goals for students, parents, families, and the community included increases in the economic attainment of adults in the community through intensified GED, college, and job training; enhanced parental involvement in all corridor schools, and decreases in violent incidents in and around schools.

Steering Committee Process

The steering committee needed to bring many local groups and organizations together to develop strategies and action plans for achieving these goals, so committee members decided to hold a series of semiannual retreats. Each retreat involved thirty-five to forty diverse individuals representing each constituency, including principals, deans, teachers, parents, hospital and clinic administrators, superintendents, doctors, district office supervisors, police officers, social workers, professors, college presidents, and business executives. This large group was divided into several subcommittees, which developed action plans in the broad areas of instructional practice, innovative programs, health issues, parental involvement, and grade articulation and transfer. Action plans were written and submitted for critique and approval by the large group. They delineated specific activities, timelines for activity completion, persons responsible for completion, necessary funding sources, and methods to evaluate the activities' successes and failures.

The retreats have also been opportunities for corridor cooperation. For example, at one retreat the Roosevelt High School principal voiced to the intermediate school principal her concern that entering freshmen come to high school with many writing deficiencies that inevitably retard their academic progress. The two principals then developed a strategy to address the problem by designing an after-school bridging program. Eighth graders would take classes at Roosevelt from 3:00 to 5:00 P.M. two days a week and study with a high school writing teacher. This would permit students to experience the academic levels of writing expected at the next level and would help them become acclimated to the culture of high school.

However, two parent representatives, although pleased with the idea of the Academic Bridge Program, were concerned with the students' safety. The parents felt that the eighth graders might not be mature enough to travel home alone at 5:00 P.M. during the winter months, when it becomes dark at an early hour. The Bronx Community College dean in the group immediately offered the solution of using the college buses that transport students from the campus to the local subway station at night. One bus could be rerouted to Roosevelt High School at 5:00 P.M. to transport the I.S. 82 bridge program students back to their intermediate school, where their parents could meet them and escort them home safely.

The development of this program deepened the emerging collaboration by helping the partners experience the benefits of consultation and joint problem solving. It also underscored that all corridor students, regardless of their age or educational level, are the responsibility of all of the institutional partners.

Strategies and Outcomes

During the first four years of the corridor initiative, the steering committee developed several highly innovative strategies to address a variety of corridor educational, social, and health needs. The corridor initiative has had noteworthy results in the short term and has tremendous potential for ongoing implementation in the future. The following examples represent selected strategies and activities created by corridor constituents that have produced measurable results.

Fridays at the College Program. In 1994, my Bronx Community College colleagues and I collaborated with I.S. 82 personnel to develop an innovative weekly enrichment program on the college campus for seventh and eighth graders at the intermediate school. The program provides minority middle school students access to the educational opportunities of a community college, taking advanced classes and attending special events unavailable to them at their regular school.

A learning environment has been designed so the college can respond appropriately to the developmental needs of these adolescent students. As part of the Leadership and Community Service Academy at I.S. 82, seventh and eighth grade students and their core subject teachers spend each Friday on the Bronx Community College campus. The students take classes in a variety of subjects (for example, chemistry, biology, computer science, music and chorus, historical studies, drama and opera) taught by their core subject teachers and selected Bronx Community College professors, with college students assisting. In addition, students participate in advisory or group guidance sessions in which they discuss the many social issues, such as substance abuse, violence, and teen pregnancy, that have a significant impact on their lives. The students also explore their career aspirations and the educational preparation needed to fulfill their goals.

The enrichment of the Fridays at the College Program is pivotal to the corridor. Middle school and college personnel contend that this program has been a powerful force to counter the risks that prevent intermediate school students' academic and personal success. The intermediate school teachers report that their students are more purposeful academically when they study at the college on Fridays. The students are more serious, attentive, and motivated; they strive for and have begun to achieve higher academic standards during the week. They become extremely interested in attending college in the future as a result of their weekly experiences on campus, meeting and hearing from college personnel and associating with the college students who assist their teachers in the enrichment classes.

The Friday program has also affected the intermediate school teachers. It has given them the opportunity to team teach, with college personnel or one another, and to offer subjects outside their own disciplines. For example, the math teacher offers a course in historical studies, the English teachers offer a course in computer literacy, and the social studies teacher offers a course in music appreciation and chorus. Furthermore, the intermediate school teachers have taken the leadership in designing, implementing, and evaluating this innovative program.

Cross-Age Tutoring. In 1995, my Bronx Community College colleagues and I joined with seven core subject teachers at Roosevelt High School to establish an on-site mini-school-within-a-school, the Education and Human Services Academy. For this academy, the teachers recruited incoming freshmen interested in pursuing a career in teaching or human services. These students are trained by a reading specialist from one of the corridor elementary schools in the techniques of teaching and tutoring reading to first through fifth graders. The specialist also conducts separate training sessions for the students' teachers, to enable them to support their students' tutoring activities. As a result, twenty-five to thirty Roosevelt High School students, accompanied by their teachers from the Education and Human Services Academy, engage in cross-age reading tutorials throughout the school year with about sixty children in the three corridor elementary schools. Both the Roosevelt students' own teachers and the elementary school personnel report that the students, for the most part, evidence mature behavior and serve as excellent academic and social role models for the elementary school children. The elementary principals also insist that the cross-age tutoring has contributed to an overall increase in their students' standardized test scores in reading, with an average corridorwide increase of 8.5 percent at the elementary level.

I.S. 82 students and corridor elementary parents have also participated in tutoring elementary school children in reading. The corridor steering committee plans to expand the tutorial program so it can provide college students to tutor high school students, and high school students to tutor intermediate students in the coming school year.

Cross-Level Staff Development. Three subcommittees of the steering committee—reading, math/science, and articulation—accepted the charge of strengthening instructional practices throughout corridor schools. Each group devised its own strategy to provide additional professional development opportunities for faculty in the corridor schools.

The reading subcommittee proposed that Bronx Community College offer a tuition-free reading methods and materials course to kindergarten through eighth grade teachers in corridor elementary and intermediate schools. I therefore hired a principal and her reading specialist from a neighboring high-performing school to teach the course. Held at I.S. 82 to provide easy access for corridor teachers, the course proved to be a great success with the teachers and paraprofessionals that attended. Not only did they receive advanced pedagogy to strengthen the process of reading instruction in their schools but they were also able to begin formulating a common approach to literacy development throughout the corridor schools. The increase in standardized scores of corridor students during this period is attributable in part to the teachers' advanced training. Future plans include a kindergarten through twelfth grade approach to literacy instruction, designed by corridor educators, to ensure continuity as corridor students move from level to level.

The corridor initiative also sponsored a team of elementary reading specialists who trained forty Roosevelt teachers from all subject areas in the fundamentals of reading instruction for pre-primer and nonreaders. In large part because of the high number of low-performing students in reading at Roosevelt, the school had been placed on the state's SURR (Schools Under Registration Review) list. The elementary reading specialists also assisted the high school teachers in preparing their students for standardized secondary level reading tests. The premise of the training was "each teacher a Reading teacher." The original forty who were trained then served as turnkey trainers for their colleagues.

In large part Roosevelt High School personnel attribute the overall improvement in their students' standardized test scores in reading—a 12.8 percent increase in 1994–95 and a 7 percent increase in 1995–96—to the corridor-sponsored training. Moreover, Roosevelt's graduation rate improved 5.6 percent during this period. As a result, in spring 1996, Roosevelt became the first New York City high school in recent history to be removed from the state roster of failing schools.

In an additional corridor-sponsored activity for professional development, Roosevelt and Taft High School science and math supervisors have facilitated science and math training sessions for elementary and intermediate school teachers. In the future, these high school supervisors plan to develop their science and math workshops into three-credit courses that Bronx community college can then offer to corridor elementary school teachers.

Finally, corridor educators plan an all-day conference in the fall of 1998 to articulate the newly devised New York City academic standards in all subject areas at all grade levels. In this way, corridor educators can better coordinate their academic expectations of and practices with students from elementary through college levels.

School-Based Clinic. The corridor steering committee was greatly concerned about the many health problems experienced by students and their families in the community. As a result, it formed a subcommittee whose primary charge was to promote the social, emotional, and physical health of the children and families in the corridor schools.

Because both the high schools in the corridor initiative had already established health clinics in their buildings, the clinic subcommittee decided to facilitate the creation of a similar clinic at I.S. 82. The ultimate goal is to open the clinic not only to I.S. 82 students but to their families and also to children and their families from the elementary schools that feed into I.S. 82. This clinic, modeled after the facility at Roosevelt High School, is sponsored by a local health care partner, Morris Heights Health Center, which provided an architect to design the facility, equipment to service the students and their families, and medical personnel to run the clinic.

Initially, over 800 students were screened for dental work during the 1995–96 school year, and over 500 students were served in the clinic during the first full year of operations in that same school year. As of November 1996, over 650 students were currently being served in the comprehensive school-based clinic. The HIV/AIDS counselor has an active enrollment of affected students who receive regular counseling. The center is actively assisting young people to become fully functioning adults able to deal with conflict, to make good decisions about their bodies, relationships, educational futures, and the achievement of their dreams. Treatment of the high number of cases of asthma and poor nutrition among students at I.S. 82 is a top priority. The need to expand to offer medical services to siblings and families of students is currently under examination, in an effort to promote wellness within the corridor community.

Parental Involvement. The subcommittee on parental involvement accepted the charge of increasing corridor parents' educational, language development, and job-training opportunities as well as increasing the parents' participation in the instructional process of their children's schools. The subcommittee met with representative corridor parents, and the critical needs of such families and the experience of school officials in dealing with parents who face difficulties they are incapable of handling led to the vision of a Family Assistance Center. The subcommittee then established this center at I.S. 82 and developed plans to expand services to parents from the feeder elementary schools as well.

Initially, parents held workshops on health issues, housing, and juvenile delinquency. Now an educational component has also started, with high school equivalency, English as a Second Language, and citizenship classes held weekly. Craft and sewing classes have been added, meeting daily in the afternoon. In 1996–97, enrollment was sustained at approximately twenty-five parents on a monthly basis. The center has also assisted parents by escorting them to various government agencies to seek support in solving their problems.

Lessons Learned

An assessment of corridor activities and accomplishments permits us to draw a number of conclusions about the nature of collaboration, learning, and leadership in an initiative of this magnitude. First of all, true collaboration exists and sustains itself continually when the following processes occur:

Participant identification and affiliation across organizations is nurtured.
Continual formal and informal communication among participants is maintained.
Participants across institutions, organizations, grade levels, and subject matter areas share a common vision.
There is evidence of trust among participants across participating organizations.

Second, cross-institutional learning has been enhanced as a result of the corridor initiative. Both teachers and administrators feel greatly empowered by acquiring contextual knowledge about the cultures and expectations of the school levels prior to and subsequent to their own.

Educators feel that their effectiveness has also been enhanced by their participation in the systematic opportunities provided by the corridor initiative for articulation with colleagues throughout the grade levels, kindergarten to college. These opportunities have included the following:

High school teachers have accompanied their students to corridor elementary schools for cross-age tutoring.
Elementary math and science teachers have gone to corridor high schools to receive in-service training from the high school math and science department chairs.
In the Fridays at the College Program, intermediate school teachers have taught at Bronx Community College, capitalizing on the modern facilities and intellectual climate of the campus to demonstrate enhanced creativity, risk taking, and autonomy.
Students of all ages have exhibited positive changes in behavior. They are exceedingly purposeful when taken to an educational institution beyond their own grade level: for example, elementary school students to the Fridays at the College Program, intermediate school students to the high school bridge program, and high school students to college orientation and special events.

Through collaborative planning and communication across disciplines, grades, levels, and sectors, educators are able to take pride in their contributions to the common effort. In turn, collaborative inquiry between teachers and university-based researchers provides a number of benefits. It creates opportunities for sharing information and for learning from one another at different levels in the educational system. It increases the resources—human, financial, material, and technical—available to individuals, and holds promise for solving problems and improving schools (Smith and Knight, in press; Rosenholtz, 1989; Francis, Hirsch, and Rowland, 1994).

Third, the corridor initiative demonstrates ways to evolve and sustain effective leadership by nurturing multiple leaders and providing numerous leadership opportunities for diverse participants, students and faculty alike. Wheatley (1992) emphasizes this relational dimension of leadership: "Leadership is always dependent on the context, but the context is established by the relationships we value. We cannot hope to influence any situation without respect for the complex network of people who contribute to our organizations" (pp. 144–145). The corridor initiative has affirmed opportunities to honor and value the diverse contributions of its participants and the leadership abilities of educators, administrators, parents, and health care and social service providers by assigning traditional leadership roles to facilitate corridor activities and by creating, through subcommittee membership, roles, expectations, and viable opportunities for a multitude of individuals to apply new leadership skills and perspectives.

Of course problems persist that once solved will help the corridor initiative run more smoothly. These problems are the need for each corridor partner to effect financial institutionalization of corridor activities within its organization, the need for all corridor professionals to integrate fully the initiative's activities with their daily work activities, and the need for corridor professionals from kindergarten to twelfth grade to be able to implement corridor activities without always relying on facilitation from Bronx Community College. To address these issues, I continue to bring corridor participants together for periodic workshops and focus groups to plan their strategies for greater financial, programmatic, and managerial autonomy.

Ellen Schnepel, the external evaluator of the project during the 1996–97 academic year, offers a perspective that captures the spirit of the initiative. She maintains that the corridor initiative shows that student achievement, academic preparation, and personal attainment improve as school leaders undertake multiple systemic efforts that involve a collaborative and holistic approach to effect educational reform. As Schnepel (1997) sees it, the corridor initiative does not promote isolated programs for small groups of students. Instead, the collaborative relationships fostered by the initiative permit the development of a series of programs between and within schools at different levels in the total system—elementary, middle, and high school and community college—affecting a large number and variety of students. Such an initiative cannot but have an impact on the whole system, and it will achieve increasingly positive and sustainable outcomes over time and across institutions. Finally, Schnepel contends that contrary to viewing at-risk children and youths in Bronx neighborhoods as lost causes, the corridor initiative promotes the view that every student deserves a fair chance to reach his or her potential, amid conditions of hope, trust, and support.

References

Francis, S., Hirsch, S., and Rowland, E. "Improving School Culture Through Study Groups." *Journal of Staff Development*, 1994, *13*, 12–13.

Rosenholtz, S. *Teachers' Workplace: The Social Organization of Schools*. White Plains, N.Y.: Longman, 1989.

Schnepel, E. M. *Final Report of the Bronx School Leaders Project*. New York: Bronx Community College, 1997.

Smith, R. G., and Knight, S. L. In R. Sinclair and W. Ghory (eds.), *Reading and Teaching All Students: Excellence with Decency for All*. Thousand Oaks, Calif.: Corwin Press, in press.

Wheatley, M. *Leadership and the New Science*. San Francisco: Berrett-Koehler, 1992.

MICHAEL C. GILLESPIE is associate professor of education and senior director of collaborative programs, Bronx Community College.

Community colleges in rural areas can play a critical role in developing collaborations and relationships that link educational access and economic development.

The Role of Rural Community Colleges in Expanding Access and Economic Development

Héctor Garza, Ronald D. Eller

As rural America prepares for the twenty-first century, community colleges are being challenged to play new roles as catalysts for local and regional development. In addition to their traditional roles in prebaccalaureate education, these colleges are now being asked to reach out to previously underserved populations and to provide leadership for the revitalization of community and regional economies as well. The rural community college of the future will be much more than a place where people go to take college courses. It will be an indispensable part of the community's overall efforts to build a better future for all of its citizens. The best of these colleges will be at the center of these efforts to improve community life.

The new economic environment of the next century, for example, calls for the greater use of technology, lifelong learning, educational flexibility, long-term planning, and community-based strategies for growth, and community colleges are ideally situated to provide leadership for this transformation. Especially in severely distressed rural areas, the community college is often the institution best capable of initiating and nurturing the local partnerships and regional collaborations that can find solutions for critical community problems.

The Rural Community College Initiative is a program designed to assist colleges in some of America's most severely distressed rural areas to design locally effective practices that facilitate this transformation of the college and the community. Through this initiative, the Ford Foundation seeks to encourage colleges to establish sustainable programs that increase access to higher education for traditionally underserved and disadvantaged populations and that foster economic development in rural areas.

Background and Context

In 1992, the Education, Media and Culture and the Asset Building and Community Development Programs of the Ford Foundation began exploring the feasibility of a collaborative initiative to improve the institutional capacities of rural community colleges to act as catalysts for change in their communities and regions. In hopes of gaining further insights about rural community colleges, the foundation funded several studies that described the institutional contexts of rural community colleges serving economically distressed areas. These studies clarified the needs and challenges of these institutions and identified ways the foundation could be of assistance to them.

Energized by the findings and the prospects of developing a collaborative program between two distinct but related program areas, access to higher education and economic development, the two Ford program directors began to build a new collaborative paradigm in grantmaking and program management. The story of the emerging collaborative model goes like this: two program officers representing two different divisions at the Ford Foundation identified rural community colleges as key institutions that could enhance both educational and economic opportunities in economically distressed regions. The feasibility of collaborating on the conceptualization, design, and funding of this initiative was discussed and agreed on, especially the need to see these twin goals as interdependent. Together, the program officers convened a small group of community college leaders and rural economic development specialists to help them think through some of the opportunities and challenges faced by rural community colleges. Through this collaborative and consultative process, an initiative framework was developed with broadly defined goals "to increase the capacity, visibility, and resources of rural community colleges."

In 1993, the program officers invited MDC, Inc., a research and technical assistance organization dedicated to rural employment and economic development, to assist them in the continued design and management of the Rural Community College Initiative (RCCI). This work used a collaborative and consultative process, benefiting from the increased talents and expertise of the expanded team. Together, the Ford Foundation and MDC staff developed a conceptual framework for the initiative and defined it as a "work in progress," to be refined as new stakeholders were invited to participate.

The operative assumption underlying RCCI is that given the necessary resources (planning time and technical assistance, collaboration among colleagues, and availability of modest grant funds), rural community colleges in the most persistently poverty-stricken regions of the country can increase access to higher education and serve as a catalyst for economic development, thereby helping the poor to become more economically independent and helping local economies become more competitive.

In 1994, a grant was awarded to MDC to plan and administer a pilot program involving nine rural community colleges located in geographically diverse and economically distressed counties. The first round of institutions selected to participate included Alabama Southern Community College (Alabama Black Belt), Coahoma Community College (Mississippi Delta), Hazard Community College (eastern Kentucky), Northern New Mexico Community College, Southeast Community College (eastern Kentucky), Southwest Texas Junior College (Middle Rio Grande), Salish Kootenai College (western Montana), Fort Belknap College (Montana), and Fort Peck College (Montana). The RCCI grant provided the participating community colleges with financial resources, a planning process, and technical assistance aimed at building institutional capacities to respond to the twin goals of the RCCI, student access to postsecondary education and rural economic development.

MDC provided the participating institutions with a set of ongoing planning and team development activities. Following initial meetings with the college presidents to explore and refine the key goals of the demonstration project in June and August 1994, the participating colleges were invited to the first of a series of leadership institutes; this one was held in October 1994 and hosted by Southwest Texas Junior College at Uvalde, Texas. Participants attended workshops on action planning and group facilitation. In effect, each institution began a planning process resulting in a grant proposal to the Ford Foundation outlining ways each institution would expand its capacity to increase access to educational programs and to promote economic development. At this institute, participants were introduced to the *vision to action* planning process by MDC staff. This process included forming a team and holding meetings with community leaders to introduce the initiative to them and involve them in it. Through meetings and discussions held at this first institute, the participants contributed to defining the role of rural community colleges in generating access and economic development.

RCCI's long-range goal of helping the participating colleges become more effective catalysts for economic development and of assisting poor regions to move toward economic independence is integrally related to educational access because educational attainment and high poverty are barriers to regional development. MDC views the economic development objectives of community colleges as creating jobs, raising incomes, generating wealth, and reinvesting that wealth in the region's businesses, institutions, and people. To increase the stability and resilience of a regional economy, it is essential to diversify the economic base. Ideally, a community or region defines the kind of economic development it seeks in accordance with the values of its people—for instance, a community may place strong emphasis on jobs with high wages and generous benefits or on environmental protection combined with the preservation of traditional culture.

Rural community colleges generally serve a broad socioeconomic cross section of the population, and the colleges participating in the RCCI serve large numbers of the poor. There are particular populations, however, that face special barriers to education and employment; they are the people for whom college is often an alien idea and a forbidding institution. RCCI hopes to change this trend through the way MDC defines the role of community colleges in access, as not just providing passive accessibility through open admissions and low tuition but engaging in active, aggressive outreach, counseling, support, and job placement; building partnerships with secondary schools; recruiting high school drop-outs, welfare mothers, and other disadvantaged adults and youth for college programs and establishing programs that enable them to succeed; ensuring that adult literacy programs are accessible, of high quality, and helpful in preparing adults for the workplace; acting as a one-stop center that provides or refers students to all the educational, employment, and training services that an unemployed adult or youth may need; building partnerships with universities to ensure that community college students can transfer successfully; and offering distance learning opportunities.

As part of their planning activities, participating institutions visited sites with noteworthy programs to gain familiarity with innovative approaches to access and economic development issues. In February 1995, at the institute hosted by Northern New Mexico Community College, participants briefed one another on the insights gained through these visits. A major focus of this institute was to move the colleges from force-field analyses to project development and grant writing. It was also at this institute meeting that the Ford Foundation announced the participation of the American Council on Education and the role the council would have in conducting RCCI documentation and assessment.

The documentation and assessment component of the Rural Community College Initiative provides a mechanism for

Documenting the processes used by the participating rural community colleges in order to glean the "lessons learned" from each situation and to use this information in subsequent program planning and replication initiatives

Validating the appropriateness and effectiveness of specific program interventions and implementation strategies and documenting lessons learned and effective practices to be used in the next phase of the RCCI

Identifying and evaluating strategies and practices related to improving access to higher education for the underserved and undereducated in rural settings

Identifying and evaluating strategies and practices related to the role of rural community colleges as catalysts for improving local economies through economic development initiatives

Using the data collected through the assessment work to promote institutional change in rural community colleges as they become engaged in rural economic development initiatives; sharing the results with other rural community college practitioners, local and regional economic development councils, and key policymakers who help shape programs, policies, and practices that have an impact on these colleges and their communities

Using a case study approach, each of the four documentation specialists hired to conduct the assessment work made several visits to at least two of the community college campuses to capture an initial qualitative portrait of the participating institutions. The basic unit of analysis was the rural community college. Using standardized interview protocols and field observation guides, these research specialists examined, described, analyzed, and reported on a variety of regional characteristics and institutional factors including programs and facilities, student and faculty demographics and characteristics, institutional and organizational structures, procedural and developmental processes, campus climates and their impact on students, and linkages with local and county groups, schools, and agencies.

Questions related to the Rural Community College Initiative program goals and institutional objectives and strategies were also incorporated into the interview and field observation instrument. The specialists collected data through structured interviews with students, faculty and staff, local residents, and community and business leaders to capture a diversity of voices, opinions, and visions, thereby creating a reasonably complete local and institutional portrait. The words and numbers were analyzed, compared, and contrasted to identify recurring themes, trends, and institutional similarities and differences and to assess individual and institutional capacities to respond to the challenges posed by the RCCI.

These findings were detailed in several reports submitted to the foundation and were used to develop generalizations for future empirical research. They also assisted the team in modifying and refining the assessment process for continuous quality improvement, identified research questions for future research, and assisted MDC and the Ford Foundation to refine the operating assumptions, program principles, and management practices for the next phase of the Rural Community College Initiative. Moreover, this effort documented institutional capacities and needs and offered recommendations for going to scale.

In 1996, the nine original colleges received funding from the Ford Foundation to implement the projects designed during the planning stage of the RCCI. In addition the foundation invited another fifteen community colleges to participate in a second round of the program. The documentation team continued to follow the progress of the nine pilot colleges in order to identify lessons learned from the implementation of these demonstration projects for other rural institutions. The results of this assessment research were released in a series of reports in 1998 by the American Association of Community Colleges (Eller and others, 1998a, 1998b).

Redefining Access

Rural community colleges have traditionally based their mission on the philosophy of open access to higher education. However, colleges serving distressed areas face special challenges because their students must cope with geographic distances, poor preparation for college, weak economies, and inadequately trained workforces. Reaching those who face these special barriers to education and employment, therefore, requires colleges to move beyond traditional open-door strategies for increasing access and to provide aggressive outreach and support services to the disadvantaged. RCCI colleges have endeavored to address this special need through a variety of new campus programs.

Common to many rural distressed areas, for example, is a fragmentation of private and public agencies that makes it difficult to create real partnerships that address community problems such as school drop-out rates, welfare reform, job creation and retraining, and adult education. Yet limited local resources demand collaboration if aggressive strategies to improve educational levels and workforce skills are to succeed. All of the RCCI institutions have developed projects that encouraged college-community partnerships designed to improve the transition from high school to college, enhance workplace performance, and increase opportunities for advancement.

Southeast Community College and three local school systems, for instance, established a partnership that created a joint college-community early intervention program for eighth graders that promises them a scholarship to college on graduation from high school. Southwest Texas Junior College created similar partnerships with twenty-one local districts. These partnerships employ the Internet and videoconferencing to give high schools access to academic offerings hitherto unavailable to them, especially to those experiencing financial hardships. Other RCCI colleges have initiated collaborations with local industries to establish campus-based technical training centers that minimize the effects of downsizing and provide management training and other on-site educational services to local workers. Such centers help link the college with business and industry in the area and serve as a gateway to students' enrollment in additional programs at the college. These partnerships go beyond emergency and short-term training programs to establish more permanent relationships among colleges, public schools, and business and industry, and they help create a culture of collaboration that is critical to successful community development.

A second strategy employed by the colleges has been to increase distance, or off-campus, learning opportunities and thus improve access for remote communities. Geographic distance and insufficient transportation often make it difficult for rural individuals with family and work responsibilities to pursue higher education. Branch campuses and extended campus centers can provide basic education and core coursework, but their range of offerings is often limited. Recent advancements in telecommunications technology, however, make it possible to improve the delivery of a broader curriculum not only at the main campus but to remote sites as well. A number of RCCI colleges have responded by expanding their distance education technologies. These initiatives have included new partnerships with regional colleges and universities to deliver electronic coursework as well as the expansion of remote telecommunications facilities.

To improve retention and successful employment among disadvantaged students, several colleges have enhanced or restructured the educational support services available on campus. Alabama Southern Community College, for example, restructured its developmental studies program to enhance faculty abilities to diagnose student deficiencies and provide both personal and instructional support. In so doing, it has changed the face of instruction at the college as well, revolutionizing the use of computers and linking student evaluation tools with new counseling, advising, and teaching strategies. By integrating basic skills, student support services, and adult education, Alabama Southern has facilitated a paradigm shift from teaching to learning that has greatly reduced student attrition and enhanced student attitudes toward learning. This approach to developmental studies has energized the faculty, raised the bar on faculty performance expectations, and generally transformed the teaching and learning process on the campus as a whole.

Finally, several RCCI colleges have emphasized the development of a variety of holistic approaches to access, reaching out broadly to recruit and support underserved populations such as high school drop-outs, welfare parents, and other disadvantaged adults. For many rural residents, accessing the opportunities available through higher education requires overcoming a number of noneducational barriers. Low family income, lack of child-care services, health problems, inadequate transportation, and customs and attitudes that do not promote education can prevent men and women from achieving productive employment or pursuing further education. To better serve these disadvantaged students, RCCI colleges have initiated a variety of academic, noncredit, and family support programs designed to reach the individual throughout life and within the context of his or her family and community.

At Southwest Texas Junior College and at Northern New Mexico Community College, newly established day-care programs make it easier for parent students to attend classes and also provide their children with significant early socialization experiences. One tribal college, Fort Peck, established a center for family and community services that offers a range of noncredit programs for welfare recipients, teen parents, young families, displaced adult workers, potential farmers and ranchers, recovering substance abusers, and many other clients. Workshops on domestic abuse, dysfunctional families, grief recovery, staying sober, communicating with teachers, and other subjects attract people to participate in programs that can last the whole day long. Such programs not only address a variety of family and community barriers to employment and education but create an image of the college as a caring place for everyone and serve as a gateway to other educational opportunities.

The experiences of the RCCI pilot institutions suggest that improving economic opportunities for minority populations in rural distressed areas requires colleges and communities to reexamine their traditional assumptions about access. Strategies appropriate for urban and suburban areas may be inadequate for rural communities. The challenges of rural geography, culture, income, and history dictate that open-admissions strategies and enrollment-driven programming will be insufficient to meet the needs of these communities in the twenty-first century. Just as an effective curriculum for rural students includes a *pedagogy of place* and appropriate economic development for rural areas is place specific, strategies to improve access to higher education must look toward the community and toward the context of that place.

Redefining the meaning of access within the academic culture of the campus and within the community as a whole is the critical first step to building more effective access strategies. This means not only the reeducation of faculty and administrative staff but also the implementation of a variety of creative programs and practices that reach students where they live and encourage both personal and family growth. Such practices include the expansion of traditional educational services through new technologies, distance learning, work-site training, developmental coursework, and scholarship assistance and also the provision of a more comfortable and place-sensitive learning environment that values local culture.

Moreover, to reach rural populations that have historically faced barriers to employment and education, RCCI colleges are moving beyond traditional roles and delivery systems to address noneducational issues such as child care, transportation, and family and personal development. Just as educational reform in rural secondary schools is placing greater emphasis on parent involvement, student nutrition, after-school programs, transportation services, and interactive learning, these rural colleges are developing family-based approaches to learning, including the initiation of partnerships with schools and other social agencies committed to this goal. And just as many new businesses are finding ways to support the educational and personal growth of employees in order to increase productivity, colleges are learning how to support the entire individual within his or her family and community context in order to improve academic success.

Rural Economic Development

Improving access to higher education, however, does not in itself ensure community economic prosperity unless that access is linked to an expanding local economic environment. In rural distressed areas, improving economic opportunities requires more than the traditional job creation activities that have characterized development efforts in the past. Challenges of geography and infrastructure, poor social services and inadequate education, and historical patterns of exploitation have left these regions dependent and without the human and civic capital to build a sustainable economy. The politics of race, class, and ethnicity have burdened their development in ways different from that of suburban America.

One of the distinguishing characteristics of the economies of rural distressed areas, for example, is the relative absence of indigenous entrepreneurs and the paucity of capital available for development. Yet in rural areas where there are few midsized or large employers, small business development presents one of the greatest opportunities for economic growth. As a result of the RCCI, many of the participating colleges have established or expanded small business development centers that offer training and technical support to local entrepreneurs. These centers work with local residents and students to design business plans and marketing strategies and to create a positive entrepreneurial climate in the community. Southeast Community College in Kentucky also collaborated with five local banks to establish a revolving loan fund, the Pine Mountain Development Corporation, which provides startup and expansion capital for local small businesses that is not otherwise available.

Along with many suburban community colleges, RCCI campuses have also reached out to existing businesses and industries to establish partnerships for workforce development. These partnerships provide opportunities for basic education and advanced technical training for existing workers and organizational training for management. Alabama Southern's partnership with the Ciba Chemical Company offers a formula of scholarships, internships, and employment possibilities that provides a promising model. This training program supports local industry needs and gives twenty scholarships annually to local students. The college has also established a partnership with Auburn University to create the Center for Excellence in Forestry, Paper and Chemical Technology, which serves local industries through technical training and technology transfer.

The most effective practices among RCCI institutions, however, go beyond traditional workforce training alliances with businesses and industries, although these are important, to enhance indigenous entrepreneurial development and civic capacity. These practices recognize the cultural differences within communities and build on the cultural assets of minorities, working-class people, and the poor to develop culturally appropriate curricula and support programs. Such efforts succeed when the college is an integral part of the whole community and not responsive to just one element of that community.

Tribal colleges, perhaps as a result of their unique situation, offer excellent examples of this integration. Set up to be integral parts of the community culture, they are able to reach out to catalyze the intended change in economic and community vitality. Business and economic assistance centers on tribal campuses give close attention to the incorporation of Indian values and the traditions of the locality in entrepreneurial training. They build economic capacity out of community strengths rather than deficiencies and promote economic self-determination without destroying traditional culture. The regional vocational training program at Northern New Mexico Community College offers another example. In a unique program the college emphasizes traditional Chicano arts and crafts and also has expanded marketing opportunities for local craftspeople by creating an artisan database.

Currently not all aspects of local cultures will contribute to building a dynamic economy. Partnerships and collaboration are absolutely necessary for effective community development, but organizations and agencies serving distressed rural communities often have little historical experience of working together and creating sustainable partnerships. The political culture in these communities does not support an environment of cooperation within bureaucracies and across class and racial lines. To change this situation, RCCI colleges are helping to build a culture of cooperation in their communities by modeling effective access and economic development partnerships themselves and by facilitating leadership development and networking among leaders within their regions. For instance, several of the pilot RCCI colleges have established regional leadership development programs and initiated regional strategic planning dialogues among businesses, agencies, and local governments. Southwest Texas now sponsors a regional case competition that encourages university business students to propose alternative strategies for the economic development of the area, which are then considered by local leaders at an annual conference.

The RCCI experience suggests, moreover, that community colleges can play an important role in developing collaborations and relationships among rural agencies and businesses, but building a cooperative environment requires time, leadership, and political skill. Effective practice requires that the college president maintain an active role on state and regional economic development boards, commissions, and other development organizations, and that college faculty come to view participation in the civic life of the community as an extension of their role in the classroom.

Finally, RCCI colleges have learned that transforming the rural community college into a catalyst for economic development is a long-term process rather than a list of model projects or a lockstep strategy for change. Rural communities differ dramatically, and RCCI does not impose a particular set of programs or strategies to solve regional problems; rather it seeks to foster a climate of innovation that will spark local solutions. In the course of the RCCI process, visions change, knowledge grows, and strategies evolve to meet new contexts and understanding. This process of transformation of the college and the community is ongoing, and campus leaders must be committed to sustaining the process as an integral part of a new institutional culture. Throughout the process, it is important to focus on projects that are achievable, that have a clear goal, and whose success can be easily measured by the faculty and the community.

Conclusion

The Rural Community College Initiative demonstrates that institutional capacity for increasing access to economic opportunities for previously underserved populations can be expanded through a heavy injection of new ideas and higher expectations for institutional efforts. All nine pilot campuses are much more visible in their communities as a result of their involvement in the RCCI than they were before it. Interaction with their communities has increased collaborations and partnerships for change. Invigorated campus leadership has recognized that there is a tremendous need for leadership development in the local community as well. To varying degrees the nine RCCI pilot colleges have adopted a community-based framework for improvement, as opposed to an institutionally based approach.

RCCI has helped its member colleges, moreover, to move beyond simply preparing students for jobs or migration out of their communities. Increasingly, these colleges are taking an active role in creating environments that promote the sustainable, long-term economic development that allows students to remain and work in their communities if they wish. Although they differ in their strategies and the maturity of their processes, most of these colleges are building connections between traditional culture and contemporary society and between individuals and the community. In so doing they are becoming part of a comprehensive social force directed at broad-based community renewal that empowers individuals with the means to discover their own talents and to go beyond survival and to thrive.

References

Eller, R., Garza, H., Martinez, R., Pace, C., and Pavel, M. *Access to Rural Community Colleges: Removing Barriers to Participation.* Washington, D.C.: American Association of Community Colleges, 1998a.

Eller, R., Garza, H., Martinez, R., Pace, C., and Pavel, M. *Economic Development and Rural Community Colleges: Learning from the Rural Community College Initiative.* Washington, D.C.: American Association of Community Colleges, 1998b.

HÉCTOR GARZA *is vice president of the Division of Access and Equity Programs at the American Council on Education.*

RONALD D. ELLER *is director of the Appalachian Center at the University of Kentucky.*

The community college needs a new partnership paradigm. Central to this paradigm are the modeling of collaborative relationships, an emphasis on student development, the development of community partnerships, and the creation of new forms of planning and resource allocation.

The Partnership Paradigm: Collaboration and the Community College

Sara Lundquist, John S. Nixon

The period of the 1980s was a tumultuous one for the city of Santa Ana, the urban center of Orange County, California. A significant population increase, largely fueled by growth in the immigrant population, collided with a massive shift in the Southern California economy, placing new challenges on the city's infrastructure and educational system. Explosive growth among the school-age and English language learning populations, combined with rapidly changing technology in the workplace, required a number of the city's leading institutions to cooperate more closely or face losing the quality of life they valued and the economic stability required to maintain it.

In response to this constellation of forces, the CEOs of Santa Ana's leading institutions came together in 1989 to form Santa Ana 2000, an interagency collaborative designed to maximize cooperative planning and problem solving citywide. A preexisting K–16 collaborative, Project STEP, led by the University of California, Irvine, had built strong relationships among the local educational partners, including the community college and the school district, and had already established a focus on intersegmental strategies that could assist at-risk and underrepresented students to complete high school successfully and enter postsecondary education. A number of challenges relating to resources, capacities, curriculum, and pedagogy emerged as these collaborative entities joined forces to combat the growing threat of educational underachievement. Key challenges included the defunding of public education in California, school overcrowding, high student-teacher ratios, poverty, the lure of gangs and drugs, a recessionary and changing economy, a new majority of English language learning students entering local schools, and a higher education system unprepared to welcome and successfully support the new generation of students it was beginning to receive.

At Santa Ana College, severe budget constraints, level enrollment, and a growing discrepancy between the demographics of the surrounding community and the college's student population served as warning signals that significant change was needed in the college's structure and programs if the college was to embrace and serve the surrounding community.

Reorganizing for Collaboration

The initial organizational response, undertaken by the chancellor, was a complete reorganization of the college's administrative structure, realigning program and service affiliations within both student services and instruction and creating a new office staffed by two equivalent positions, the vice president of academic affairs and the vice president of student services. Charged with maintaining the high caliber of existing educational and support service programs, these positions also were expected to accelerate the pace of institutional innovation and work collaboratively with faculty and administrative leaders in the college, in local schools, and in surrounding universities to build enrollment as well as increase retention, graduation, and transfer. Several specific strategies were added to the institutional expectation that these two positions, and the segments of the college they represent, would collaborate closely. One strategy was the blending between these positions of primary leadership responsibility for programs traditionally located in one or the other domain. For example, the vice president of student services administers the college's future teachers program, and the vice president of academic affairs oversees the New Freshman Experience initiative.

Another strategy was to establish joint administration of numerous community-building and student activity external initiatives, including the Middle College High School, Community Outreach Partnership Centers, and summer residential programs. Last, but equal in importance, was the Student Services/Academic Affairs cochairmanship and partnership work on such college and district groups as the Welfare Reform Task Force, Joint Deans Administrative Council, Student Equity Committee, Articulation Work Groups, Enrollment Management Committee, and the joint Academic Affairs/Student Services sponsorship throughout the year of professional development activities designed to be catalysts for program or curricular change.

The realignment of the college's administrative structure and the creation of job titles for the vice presidents reflecting areas of professional emphasis rather than exclusive domains set in motion a new phase in the college's development. Central to this change has been the modeling of a collaborative culture, an emphasis on the development of student and community-focused partnerships, and support for a rethinking of assumptions about student learning and achievement. Significantly, the shift also entailed expanding the number of involved stakeholders and giving more scrutiny to actual outcomes, and it simultaneously established a new collegewide context for resource allocation and program development.

The close linkage and continual involvement of educational partners on the sending (K–12) and receiving (university) ends of the student continuum was critical in building a deeper appreciation of the preexisting restraining and enabling forces that influence important decisions about where to invest time and resources for maximum student benefit. The new culture of collaboration dramatically improved the quality of local strategic planning, as systemic data from all partners was shared and evaluated both to chart outcomes and to pinpoint barriers affecting student progress.

A New Approach to Planning and Program Development

An important, internal impact of this overall shift was the rethinking of the purpose of resource and program development. In the past such development was used primarily to address problems or meet needs that the basic system did not attend to. The new focus that emerged was both systemic and transformational. In analyzing the college's recent history with grants and other categorically funded instructional and student services programs, we realized that all too often, even when program outcomes were excellent, the efforts existed on the margins of the institution. On occasion they even discouraged individuals who would otherwise develop programs or services for students, as the special effort supplanted the core institutional function, bringing new visibility and resources to necessary work but often excluding institutional efforts already in place.

A new focus on internal coalition building at Santa Ana College was established as a result of identifying this problem and continuing to seek more systemic solutions to significant college challenges. Existing staff and other stakeholders were invited to work together, applying their experience and perspectives to some of the institution's most pressing problems and subsequently implementing strategies to address them. This not only raised morale as the appropriate stature was accorded to the current program leaders, but it also helped move some innovative work from the periphery to the core of the institution. This in turn gave limited initiatives a stronger position as pilots for potential large-scale implementation in classroom instruction or services, rather than remaining stand-alone programs with necessarily limited impact. Examples include the expansion of cohort counseling classes for incoming freshman in the New Freshman Experience program currently in place collegewide and the use of intersegmental dialogue groups among faculty in English, ESL, and mathematics to improve the matriculation process and revise the eleventh and twelfth grade curricula.

Thus collaborative and blended leadership roles with policy and budget authority can be instrumental in breaking down some of the institutional compartmentalization of programs and services. This promotes a learner-centered focus within the college and establishes a culture that encourages collective responsibility for student access, opportunity, and achievement. These qualities in an institution are an essential prerequisite to authentic and effective collaboration.

When an established institution faces the challenges outlined previously with the new organizational structure put in place, an analysis of past practices and examples of new directions show how it has dramatically reshaped itself. Previously, Santa Ana faculty and administrators had worked for years to address these challenges, primarily pursuing strategies of intervention that reflected traditional organizational structures. The English, reading, and math faculties developed separate strategies of remediation, introducing new curricula, new technologies, and new pedagogies. The counselors, transfer center specialists, and other student services staff separately developed a number of support and intervention strategies, improving and increasing tutoring and other academic support services related to transfer and student academic achievement. Although many of these efforts resulted in new student successes and some improvement in transfer rates, as separately pursued intervention strategies they also represented the status quo in college organization and planning. A look at a successful program that reflects an out-of-the-box, or nontraditional, approach to college organization demonstrates the efficacy of a new paradigm for college organization that focuses on processes encouraging the college to respond holistically to the needs and interests of students.

The Summer Scholars Transfer Institute (SSTI) was developed out of a collaborative assessment by both the internal partners of the college (academic affairs and student services) and its external partners (the local university, other community colleges, and a national foundation). The internal partners began the SSTI program by attempting to determine the barriers Santa Ana students face to university transfer. Rather than exploring this issue in the traditional, compartmentalized way, faculty and administrators representing both academic affairs and student services worked together. Through this collaborative investigation, the college partners shared their experience with students, discussing not only barriers but also ideas and practices that could promote successful transfer.

Not surprisingly, group members discovered common ground in their assessment of barriers. They agreed that chief among these barriers was that many of their students are unprepared culturally and emotionally for the world of higher education. Even though academic preparation, particularly in basic skills, was a major problem for many students, the affective issues were even more significant and almost universal. The majority of Santa Ana's traditional college-age students who aim for a baccalaureate degree are poor and have family backgrounds that are either hostile toward or unfamiliar with higher education. The faculty saw this in their classrooms, but in classes of thirty students, they could not provide sufficient individual assistance and support. In addition, both the teaching faculty and the counselors agreed that the students had difficulty forming any positive identification with the college or with other students. Clearly, ameliorating these barriers required more than adjustments to the curriculum and more than could be accomplished in a session with a counselor.

The college partners determined that students would benefit from an experience that combined the efforts of teaching faculty and counselors in the classroom and took place in a setting that encouraged the development of a learning community among students and faculty. SSTI was the result. It incorporates partnerships between discipline faculty and counselors in teaching college classes and, in collaboration with the college's university and foundation partners, features the university as the setting for the program. Thus the students experience university residential life as they also complete a transfer-level course delivered in a compressed, intensive mode over a two-week session. The discipline faculty and counselors pair up to form a team in teaching the English, geology, philosophy, political science, psychology, or history course. The residential experience includes additional student support services staff who act as teaching assistants and group and dorm leaders, providing social and academic support. The faculty also live with the students in the dorms.

The Partnership Paradigm

Now in its fifth year, with approximately one hundred students participating from the college each summer, the SSTI program has proven quite successful. The retention rates among participants are significantly higher than those among the general population of transfer students, and the fall transfer rates from Santa Ana College to universities have increased from 411 in 1990 to 639 in 1996. Of course the success of SSTI represents far more than the success of the students who have participated. The program is an example of the shift in organizational thinking that emphasizes students and their needs as the primary focus for evaluation and planning, rather than a focus on departments, programs, and services. The collaborative development of SSTI has helped break down the often competitive structures that militated against cooperation between academic affairs and student services and between *special* and *mainstream* college programs. It has promoted a collaborative model of partnership that recognizes that the whole is greater than the sum of its parts. This new partnership framework allows the faculty, staff, and administrators to eliminate organizational voids, create connections through common interests and goals, and discover new opportunities for better serving students.

The SSTI program is also an example of a seemingly paradoxical yet beneficial result of the partnership paradigm of college organization. As a strategy affecting one hundred students each summer, SSTI represents incremental change at the college. However, it also represents systemic change as well. As a product of the partnership paradigm, SSTI is symbolic of the power of collaboration and of a community college that has shifted away from a compartmentalized and often competitive framework for doing business. Systemic change is refined and reinforced by the incremental changes manifest in new collaborative programs for students.

The simultaneous systemic and incremental change that characterizes the college's partnership paradigm can also be seen in several collaborative programs created from the successes of SSTI. Building on SSTI's teacher-counselor partnership, faculty and administrators from academic affairs and student services created the New Freshman Experience program, with cohort learning communities for incoming freshman. The program combines basic skills classes with guidance classes. Students enroll as a group in, for example, an English class, a reading class, and a counseling class. The counselor attends the English class, assisting the students and co-teaching, and all three faculty meet regularly as a team to plan instruction and develop strategies to assist individual students. This structure helps students form productive, supportive relationships with the faculty and with one another. The college is now expanding this learning community concept to include content area courses, maintaining the collaboration between discipline faculty and counselors. The development of the New Freshman Experience program further institutionalized the systemic change of the partnership paradigm and represents a new, successful incremental change.

The partnership paradigm also encourages interinstitutional collaboration. We have attempted to expand the focus on students by drawing in partner institutions through several new programs. One example is the African American Achievement Program (AAAP). This program combines the learning community structure with mentoring by businesspeople, tutoring by students from partner universities, and recruiting relationships with local high schools. Now in its second year, the AAAP has demonstrated significant improvement in retention rates among African American students at the college.

As Santa Ana College institutionalizes the partnership paradigm, it recognizes that it must develop its student clientele through outreach efforts that begin with families in the city's neighborhoods. One example of this community-centered outreach work is the college's Community Outreach Partnership Centers program (COPC), funded through a grant from the Department of Housing and Urban Development. The COPC program is a partnership among Santa Ana College, the University of California, Irvine, the city of Santa Ana, the local school district, and two community-based organizations, both of which serve large numbers of poor immigrant and linguistically isolated Hispanic residents and also large numbers of children. The goal of COPC is community capacity building, with an emphasis on community asset development, leadership, workforce preparation, child care, and housing.

Within Santa Ana College, the COPC program brings together faculty and students from ethnic studies, psychology, and history, who collaborate with colleagues from the university in conducting research on community assets and needs. These faculty and students work with child development and childcare staff from the college and basic skills faculty who provide direct services in the community, along with faculty and staff from the community centers, school district, and city. All the internal and external partners are committed to increasing the number of community residents who move through the educational pipeline to postsecondary education.

Conclusion

The partnership paradigm argues for a new organizational culture in the community college. No longer viewed departmentally, the new culture of collaboration is defined by student-centered goals. This new organizational model is necessary if community colleges are to respond effectively to rapidly changing communities and to build new educational markets by reaching out to residents who may not recognize that community colleges can provide a pathway for future growth. The notion that we cannot do it alone must be applied against the traditional schism between student services and academic affairs and between the community college and other institutions in the community. The partnership paradigm promises educational benefits to the college and the community more powerful than those any single department in the college or single institution in the community can realize.

SARA LUNDQUIST is vice president of student services at Santa Ana College.

JOHN S. NIXON is vice president of academic affairs at Santa Ana College.

A community college president discusses the collaborative dimensions of her leadership role and ways that collaboration can leverage vital resources in the community.

The Collaborative Leader

Carolyn Grubbs Williams

Throughout my administrative career I have come to see collaboration as essential to the leadership role and of special benefit to the community college.

As I assumed my prior position as president of Los Angeles Southwest College (LASC), I was also involved in the development of Los Angeles Partners Advocating Student Success (LA PASS), an interinstitutional, collaborative educational reform effort funded by the Ford Foundation. That experience confirmed my sense of the importance of collaboration. It also helped clarify the vital role that community colleges can play in spanning educational systems and bringing diverse groups together to improve the educational prospects of underserved students.

The Los Angeles Community College District serves as the fiscal agent for LA PASS. When I arrived at LASC, the chancellor at that time, Donald Phelps, asked me to facilitate the process of involving partner institutions in LA PASS. I took on the assignment, working closely with Cheryl Mabey, who, during a sabbatical leave from Mount St. Mary's College, was on assignment in the office of the district's legal counsel.

The goal of the collaborative was to involve as many key institutional players as possible in focusing on ways to get more at-risk students through the educational pipeline to the baccalaureate degree. We recognized that interinstitutional collaboration faced special challenges in a city the size and complexity of Los Angeles. To begin we needed to identify the state of educational reform in the city, identify the key institutional actors, track any record of successful practices, and develop a broad-based partnership so that we could start building an efficient educational pipeline for students. We initially involved the Los Angeles Unified School District, the nine community colleges in the Los Angeles Community College District, and the area's other higher education institutions. We also involved representatives from business and from a variety of community groups, social agencies, and reform organizations.

During the planning phase the collaborative functioned as a committee of the whole. We were extremely democratic in our initial approach. We sent out letters to a variety of organizations, starting with the educational community. As groups responded, we convened weekly meetings that functioned as focus groups. Over time we developed a process that deepened commitment and broadened participation. We used meetings to clarify critical issues and identify who else should be at the table. Then we scheduled another meeting and further discussed those issues and possible directions for action. We always ended by again asking who else should be at the table. This process was based on the strategic judgment that the more inclusive we were, the better the effort would be.

This process was successful in involving a wide range of organizations. But as participation broadened, we were challenged to maintain focus on the goals of the collaborative. We responded by emphasizing four assumptions—our priority is student achievement, we should maximize participation, we cannot think in terms of discrete projects, and we need to promote cross-learning among partners and across educational sectors.

Our collective review of existing outcome data underscored the need for a collaborative K–16 approach. Data revealed wholesale hemorrhaging throughout the Los Angeles educational pipelines. For instance, less than one-half of fifth graders were proceeding on to high school; only a minority of students were enrolling in "A–F," or letter grade, college-required courses; less than 10 percent of community college students were transferring to four-year institutions. These findings confirmed our judgment that only a collaborative approach involving many organizations could possibly respond to problems on that scale. Therefore we needed to involve as many groups as possible. Moreover, to have real impact, people cannot think in terms of single, disconnected initiatives.

Using Collaboration to Facilitate Change

We saw our task as providing a forum for institutions to plan and act together to improve the functioning of the educational system at every level. The role of LA PASS was coordinating and facilitating, rather than direction setting or controlling. That worked very well for the first year. Then we began a series of geographically targeted initiatives, which again challenged our ability to maintain a common focus. Also we had to find a way to move forward with very limited funds. We responded by emphasizing the ability of the collaborative organization to leverage funds by putting people together who can generate the resources to carry out the initiatives.

We had the advantage of coming along at the right time in the life of the city, with a real clarity of motive. LA PASS began right after the 1992 Los

Angeles civil unrest, and everyone recognized how balkanized the city had become, and was concerned with rebuilding the civic infrastructure. Also there were many significant reform initiatives already underway that were not necessarily getting the visibility and support that they needed. LA PASS was able to give them a broader arena and greater visibility. This experience encouraged organizations to engage in real collaboration. Even though they had different emphases and many were working separately in the same communities, they had many common concerns. Over time, groups began to borrow approaches and highlight each other's initiatives as well as engage in some joint planning and fundraising.

One of the important lessons to be learned from this work is that a collaborative organization can maximize the impact of reform efforts by promoting coordination and providing broader exposure to previously independent initiatives. However, such coordination requires a lengthy and careful process of building trust among the partners. LA PASS had no identity independent of the collaborative, so it did not overshadow what the various institutional partners were doing. Our primary concern was to use collaborative relationships to bring people together and promote learning about effective educational approaches among the partners, so that practices and strategies benefiting students would be widely shared and disseminated.

Maximizing the Benefits of Collaboration

The development of LA PASS provides many examples of organizations' seeing the advantage of visibility and leveraging their efforts to promote educational reform. For instance, my own institution, Los Angeles Southwest College, was working with Jordan High School. We began the collaboration by inviting the principal and the department chairs to a meeting at the college, where we introduced the LA PASS initiative. As a new president, I attempted to begin the relationship by asking if the high school had issues that the college could help facilitate. A series of conversations helped us identify a number of issues that were discouraging the high school students from continuing with their education and led to the development of a new program called College as a Family Affair, in which we invited faculty, students, and their families to the college. From that activity we deepened the relationship by moving to discipline-based sessions, in which the Jordan High department chairs met with college faculty. By the time I left the college, we had involved Jordan's whole feeder pattern of schools in discussions of curriculum and faculty development. High school faculty were meeting on the campus, the high school and middle school faculty were meeting in summer institutes, and the elementary and middle school faculty were meeting.

The Los Angeles Educational Partnership (LAEP), a nonprofit organization established to promote educational reform, was working in the same community and learned of what we were doing. LAEP has long been involved in issues of faculty development and curriculum reform. We reached out to the people at LAEP, and they joined us to expand the work, bringing their considerable expertise and additional resources. One of the significant outcomes was the joint development of a summer faculty institute for LASC, Jordan High School, and Markham Middle School faculty, held on the LASC campus.

At the same time, LA PASS cultivated other partnerships focusing on different intervention strategies to accelerate student achievement. A partnership in the central city south area, for example, built on an existing collaboration between the University of Southern California and the Foshay Learning Center. Foshay is a K–12 learning center serving 120 elementary children, 2,500 middle school students, and 600 high school students. It has been restructured into a series of "academies," developed to link rigorous college prep curricula to practical school-to-work experience in the fields of finance, health, and information technology. And a partnership developed in the earthquake-damaged northeastern San Fernando Valley/Pacoima area focused on health issues and other noneducational barriers to student achievement. This decentralized approach has helped LA PASS partners see the power of cross-learning; it links educators not only across educational sectors but also across geographic clusters in the city.

Coordinating Efforts and Maintaining a Common Focus

Developing the LA PASS type of collaborative is to some extent like building a virtual organization. As we grappled with issues of coordination and focus, we were faced with a number of critical questions: How do we know we're on target? Are we engaged in the right kinds of initiatives with the right people at the table? How do we know where we're going?

Over time, we identified a set of common issues that provided the needed focus. Our first common theme was "doubling the chances for success" of at-risk students at every educational level. A common focus on that challenge helped the participants develop a number of significant initiatives. It led all the institutional partners to focus on key transition points in the educational pipeline, such as doubling the number of fifth graders proceeding to high school, doubling the number of middle school students completing algebra, doubling the number of community college students transferring to four-year institutions.

As we developed the collaborative, we also maintained an emphasis on assessment, which enhanced our credibility and helped us maintain focus because it encouraged systemic planning. The Rand Corporation offered its services to LA PASS and was very helpful in assisting us with a variety of assessment issues. We have consistently devoted attention to assessment and have worked to gather district and school-by-school data and to match state data with four-year university and Los Angeles Community College District data.

Coordination among the partner institutions was also enhanced by regular meetings, to give people a sense that they were in this together. We were careful to design meetings to ensure that people were making connections and sharing ideas. The consistency of scheduled meetings also provided continuity, keeping people involved and at the table. We had a core of people from all the groups who helped participating institutions stay focused and maintain communication.

Combining Roles

From the time I came to Los Angeles Southwest College I combined the roles of team leader of an interinstitutional collaborative and president of the college. These combined roles produced a number of advantages, and I never felt the need to sharply separate them. As president, I saw the collaborative work as part of my external efforts, knowing that the collaborative efforts would benefit the college as well as the other partners. I felt that if the college were to be successful in serving the community, it had to be part of the collaborative effort.

The collaborative work also became a real rallying point for change within the community college district. It helped identify and validate critical areas of need and became a way of leveraging grant efforts. Within my college it provided exposure for many people and helped a variety of administrators and staff build connections with counterparts in other institutions.

I have tried to continue that dual focus in my current role as president of Bronx Community College. Community colleges, to function effectively today, need to work collaboratively. They do not have the resources to fulfill their missions when they act alone. They need to pool resources and draw on the strengths of various partners to create a healthier environment for the community. However, to develop this collaborative orientation, all of us involved in community colleges need to promote a cultural change in our colleges. We need to continually educate the college about the mutual benefits of collaborative relationships. We need to be committed to staff development, but we must also build in institutional rewards and incentives to show that we value collaborative relationships. We too often look only at the academic side of what we do, at such efforts as scholarly publications and presentations. We have to create a climate where other efforts are also valued.

This year I developed a very open-ended program of faculty and staff development. In effect I have said to faculty and staff, if you have a good idea that is out of the traditional mold and will enhance what we do, submit a three-page proposal and let us fund it. I have encouraged people to take risks. Even as we recognize that not every new effort will work, we need to create climates where people are encouraged to see the mutual benefits that result from collaborating with other departments on campus and with groups in the community.

Conclusion

My experience, both in Los Angeles and in the Bronx, confirms the importance of collaboration for community colleges. The educational challenges in our cities are too vast and the resources in our individual institutions are too limited for us to act alone. The development of collaboratives provides community colleges with new opportunities to promote access and enhances the educational success of underserved students.

CAROLYN GRUBBS WILLIAMS *is president of Bronx Community College.*

The national managing partner of a multicity educational reform effort performs a number of roles that support interinstitutional collaboration.

Building Local Partnerships: Contributions of a National Center

Barbara Schaier-Peleg, Richard A. Donovan

If the 1970s were the decade when universities and colleges struggled in isolation with operational definitions of expanded access, the emphasis on articulation in the 1980s encouraged them to explore issues of access and quality with one another. The 1990s—with their focus on fuller, broader partnerships—ushered in the decade of collaboration, which as the century turns, shows no signs of abating.

The current period of collaboration has its roots in the 1980s. Despite open admissions and extensive efforts to provide new students with a wide range of support programs, community colleges became increasingly alarmed by data indicating that too few of their students—minority students in particular—were transferring to four-year colleges. Seeking solutions and prompted by grants from public and private funders, many community colleges began aggressively reaching out to neighboring four-year institutions with the intent of improving the flow of transfer students between them. In the midst of these vigorous efforts, it became clear that if the transfer pump were to be truly primed, full-scale efforts had to begin much earlier than the college years. Too often students were arriving at community colleges not only underprepared academically but with little sense of a career beyond college, let alone of why going to an unfamiliar, often unwelcoming four-year college would make much sense.

At Bronx Community College during the 1980s, our organization, Networks, began its work with partnerships by managing different interinstitutional transfer initiatives. These initiatives resulted in more academically challenging coursework; more realistic, binding articulation agreements; and improved counseling and information services. But despite these successes the transfer outcomes did not significantly improve.

NEW DIRECTIONS FOR COMMUNITY COLLEGES, no. 103, Fall 1998 © Jossey-Bass Publishers

From these initial efforts we learned that if the solutions were to be real and durable, the schools had to be engaged partners in any reform activities. Further, if communities were truly to improve linkages between different educational sectors, they had to recognize that many problems were too interrelated for educational institutions to address by themselves. Ideally, local partnerships that included not only K–16 educators but also family, community, and business representatives would give planners the resources and the momentum for a concerted effort.

In 1989, we proposed the Urban Partnership Program (UPP) to the Fund for the Improvement of Postsecondary Education and the Ford Foundation. Initially, UPP was jointly funded as a pilot project in which broad-based local collaboratives from six participating cities built on existing transfer initiatives. These partnerships developed plans to help schools and colleges work more closely together and implement organizational, curricular, and cocurricular initiatives enabling students to move less traumatically from one school to another or from one system to another. Educational reformers such as Linda Darling-Hammond (1997) make a strong case for restructuring individual schools to minimize bureaucratic intrusiveness and to liberate teachers and learners. However, even the most successfully reformed single school loses its effectiveness for children if it remains a lonely beacon for change. Improving student success requires focusing on the entire educational pipeline. Students in stimulating environs are at a serious disadvantage when they move to a new level and it turns out to be less academically challenging than the previous one and also presents no logical or organic connection with that previous one.

We hoped that by convening broad-based partnerships, UPP teams could build bridges over the chasm that frequently separates elementary from middle schools, middle schools from high schools, high schools from community colleges, and community colleges from senior colleges. At their best these collaboratively built bridges would then lead to systemwide changes. We encouraged partnerships to build on existing efforts, first, by informing themselves about other local reform activities and, second, if possible, by integrating earlier efforts into their new work. By 1991, the Ford Foundation became convinced that such partnerships could play a critical role in improving urban education and increasing baccalaureate degree attainment, so it expanded the UPP to sixteen cities and promised to support the initiative until the end of the decade.

Recognizing the complexity of the work and the challenges that individual partnerships would face, the Ford Foundation also decided that a managing partner would be essential for assisting the partnerships, updating the foundation on partnership activities, and planning for the future. As the National Center for Urban Partnerships, we became UPP's managing partner. The center's many initiatives can be grouped into five categories of support for the sixteen UPP teams scattered across the country:

The center regularly convened partnership teams so that they could support and learn from one another.

The center provided a variety of services to partnerships—training, institutes on team effectiveness, support for team leaders, and opportunities for linking people electronically via the World Wide Web and E-mail.

The center helped assess the work of each partnership through site visits and proposal reviews.

The center provided feedback to the funding agency to keep it abreast of the progress of partnerships and to identify issues of concern.

The center disseminated information through the Web and traditional print journals, and pulled together lessons gleaned from UPP.

Convener

There is a clear advantage to bringing people together who are working on similar efforts. Through large national meetings and smaller hands-on workshops and institutes—rotated among participating cities to help build local visibility and support—the consortium was strengthened as teams shared information, engaged in joint problem solving, and began to establish an environment of collegiality and trust.

During UPP's first five years, when partnership teams were smaller, the center convened national conferences twice a year. Today the center holds an annual meeting, which team leaders use to showcase and reward the work of partnership members and to introduce new partners—a school board member or a business executive, for example—to their peers in other cities, to the work of other partnerships, and to the broader partnership culture. Most participants attending these meetings for the first time are impressed with the diversity of the conferees. College presidents and school superintendents share discussions with parents, teachers, and businesspeople from across the country. The center's challenge is to create an open, interactive environment where UPP team members are introduced to best UPP practices, significant non-UPP educational reform efforts, and cutting-edge research.

At least once a year the center schedules smaller, more focused conferences. These meetings, usually thematically organized, provide partnerships the opportunity to explore key issues in depth with colleagues grappling with similar problems. They also afford the center the opportunity to help partnerships broaden their thinking and work. In March 1998, for example, the center offered a professional development symposium to strengthen the relationship between educational reform efforts and local colleges of education, particularly in the areas of preservice and in-service teacher training. Although colleges of education can be critical to school reform, many UPP cities had not actively involved them in their initial plans. But times are changing. Eugene Garcia (1998) notes the national movement from university-centered to school-centered partnerships. The professional development symposium offered a nonthreatening and focused approach to establishing a collaborative planning process between school and university leaders around an essential element of educational reform.

Pivotal to team success has been the team leader or partnership director. Few face as challenging a role as the leader who facilitates the collaborative work of multi-institutional partnerships. Such leaders have no exact counterpart and few natural allies within a partnership. Gene Maeroff (1998) identifies the higher education reward systems that offer faculty little incentive to participate fully in collaborations, the significant cultural differences between schools and colleges, and the "junior status" of precollegiate education as obstacles imped-ing collaboration and thus major challenges for partnership leaders.

It became important for the center to create forums that would allow team leaders to exchange information about partnership policy and practice. Issues such as how to deal with an uncooperative school superintendent or how best to build bridges with other local reform organizations are the concerns that UPP directors deal with on an ongoing basis. Because some team leaders already will have dealt successfully with, for example, securing institutional buy-in, they can act as resources and mentors for other leaders. As a result of such assistance, newer UPP teams can frequently develop more rapidly than their predecessors.

Provider of Services

Because multi-institutional collaboration is challenging and foreign to the way institutions typically operate, it is essential for partnerships to have time to focus on the critical yet easily avoided problems that can significantly inhibit their work. Despite the fact that most UPP partnerships scheduled planning retreats, team-managed forums were seldom able to confront or resolve the dif-ficult issues that are often roadblocks to success. In response to this challenge, we created a two-part training institute, the Institute for Effective Partnerships. First, it provides partnerships with expert assistance to work through leader-ship and communication problems, clarify and accept the roles of the diverse partners, and identify ways those partners can contribute to a shared vision. In addition to identifying and training consultants for this work, the institute, as a friendly outsider familiar with the issues, is often able to help partnerships remain focused and address priority concerns. Second, the institute focuses on defining systemic change for interinstitutional teams, helping them develop an effective planning process, and helping them work more collaboratively.

We have found technology to be an enormous resource for collaboratives, both nationally and locally. For example, the center provides electronic net-working, and the center Web site (http://www.ncup.org) includes information about what is happening within UPP and other consortia, announcements, cal-endars, bibliographies on partnership findings, funding opportunities, and the texts of key speeches—such as President Clinton's February 1998 speech on partnerships—that affect partnership work. E-mail and listservs are helping us solicit ideas for meeting agendas and special initiatives more efficiently and eco-nomically. We work closely with individual partnerships to help them set up their own listservs and reflect on how to use technology most effectively at their sites. Although technology offers partnerships significant support, without leadership and assistance most of them will be overwhelmed by it. Consequently, in 1998, we offered a training institute in conjunction with the University of Maryland to help UPP colleagues maximize their use of technology.

The center also works closely with UPP team leaders on an ongoing basis to identify and resolve local problems. On request we attend team retreats, recommend workshop facilitators and consultants, and review preliminary funding proposals. In times of crisis we tend to invite ourselves to team functions to determine the depth of the problems and suggest next steps.

Assessor of Partnership Progress

Site visits provide UPP partnerships the opportunity to showcase what they are doing and receive dispassionate feedback. Site visits also permit the center to understand better what is really happening at the institutional levels (particularly to assess the degree of local participation and buy-in) and to help initiate changes. For example, in one city we determined that the partnership was floundering because the team leader was too dominant, and we urged a more decentralized form of decision making, which the team quickly endorsed and the team leader acceded to. In another instance lack of buy-in by an influential school board member was slowing the implementation of agreed-on curricular changes. By scheduling a small working meeting with the school board member, we were able to place his city's efforts within the context of the national reform movement and win his approval.

The center reviews proposals and because of its close relationship with the partnerships can verify proposal details and help the funding agency identify issues of strength and concern. For example, we have been able to see when a proposal is too abstract to do justice to the excellent initiatives underway at ground level. Frequently cities have been successful in submitting revised proposals after receiving center feedback.

Provider of Feedback to the Funding Agency

The center interacts with the funding agency through meetings, direct conversations, and ongoing E-mail communications. We provide the agency with up-to-date information about partnership activities and specific concerns faced by teams. Generating clear RFPs is a time-consuming art, and by participating in the development of RFP guidelines, the center has been able to expedite the funder's work and head off potential problems.

During most of its UPP work, the center was fortunate in having a program officer from the funding agency who virtually became part of the center's senior staff. Not surprisingly, other senior staff at the center enjoyed unusual access to the funder and were able to participate in strategic planning often denied grantees. This led to a more coherent and fully shared vision between the funding agency, the center, and individual city partnerships.

Disseminator of Information

By working with sixteen different collaboratives in as many different cities, we have learned much about partnerships. The experiences of such a wide variety of cities have helped us identify stages of team development, strategies that lead to successful collaboration, predictable barriers, and the critical role of the team leader. Although the dissemination process is ongoing, certain activities have become routine.

Through print and electronic reports, we disseminate descriptive information quickly and broadly to all UPP participants. With a click of the mouse the latest information about national and international meetings, such as the center's summer 1998 study tour and conference in South Africa, is available.

Initially through the center magazine, *Alliance,* and later through the center Web site, information about individual partnership accomplishments and discussions about central issues reach key people in each of the UPP cities. Because the information is coming from a national organization, it is sometimes perceived as more credible than if it were only a local claim.

Special focus publications, such as case studies of the Newark Faculty Alliance, concerned with K–16 curriculum and pedagogy, or of the Santa Ana summer institute for community college students, discussed elsewhere in this volume, are also published regularly.

We organize presentations at conferences and meetings that include contrasting analyses of collaboration and reports on local efforts. Again the goal is to help the partnerships achieve greater local and national visibility.

Conclusion

The challenges that partnerships face as they try to make sustainable and systemic changes in schools, colleges, and universities should not be underestimated. Nor can educators ignore the substantial benefits that result from successful collaboration. As both a trusted ally and an outsider, the National Center for Urban Partnerships has sought to retain a focus on moving partnerships toward joining other partnerships in a larger collective as well as to provide the gentle nudges that keep individual partnerships moving toward systemic change. It is difficult to say what the results would have been if the sixteen partnerships in different cities had remained disconnected from each other throughout the years of the UPP. However, considering the variety of services the center has provided and the specific issues it has helped resolve, it seems safe to conclude that the center has made the work of the partnerships easier.

The fact that the center is located at a community college has given community colleges heightened credibility among the different cities. Although the different functions of a national managing organization are not necessarily dependent on any institutional type, most national initiatives are centered at associations or research universities. The decision by the Ford Foundation and the City University of New York to base the center at Bronx Community College sends a subtle message to prospective partners, who are frequently distracted by issues of turf and pecking order. If educators are to construct collaboratives that value and build on the strengths that each of the partnering institutions brings, it is essential that they avoid being distracted by ancient clichés.

Systemic change is slow and remains an imposing challenge. But many UPP cities are making more progress—and different types of progress—than they had made before. Teams have engaged more and more stakeholders in critical conversations and are beginning to realize the power and impact of meaningful collaboration. The role of the center is an evolving one that is sometimes filled with frustration, but watching unprecedented changes occur—and helping to influence them—is rewarding.

References

Darling-Hammond, L. *The Right to Learn: A Blueprint for Creating Schools That Work.* San Francisco: Jossey-Bass, 1997.

Garcia, E. "Collaboration in Support of Diversity: A Dean's Reflections." *On Common Ground,* 1998, *8,* 16–31.

Maeroff, G. L. "The Future of Partnerships." *On Common Ground,* 1998, *8,* 117–124.

BARBARA SCHAIER-PELEG is associate director of the National Center for Urban Partnerships.

RICHARD A. DONOVAN is director of the National Center for Urban Partnerships.

In an interview with L. Steven Zwerling, senior director, the Ford Foundation, issue editor Dennis McGrath asks about the funder's view of collaboration and the new role that is developing between funders and grantees.

Funding Collaboratives

L. Steven Zwerling

DM: Could you explain why the Ford Foundation, and other funders, have become interested in supporting collaboration? From a funder's perspective, what is different about funding a collaborative?

LSZ: All funders seem to be talking about collaboration these days, and in many ways I see this to be problematic, even though we too are encouraging and funding it. I see a lot of collaborating for the sake of collaborating, as if there is some intrinsic good in collaboration. But I'm not sure that it has intrinsic value.

I still believe in the power of individual initiative and what can be achieved by someone who has a strong sense of purpose, a vision, a mission, working alone against the currents. The paradigm-breaking individual. And so I'm skeptical about the value of a lot of the collaborative activity that is currently underway, even with support from major donors, because there are many untested hypotheses with regard to its effectiveness.

The central hypothesis is that seemingly intractable problems in education are susceptible to solution through collaboration. I do not as yet see a lot of evidence to convince me that that is in fact true. On some level, collaboration feels like the "innovation du jour." This may sound ironic since much of what I've been funding while at the Ford Foundation has been of a collaborative nature. What is critical is the evidence that convinces a funder that of all the ways that we know to approach certain problems, a collaborative approach is the best one. So, in the cases where the Ford Foundation in its education work is funding collaboration, I'm hoping that this isn't just because we see it to be the latest panacea but rather is based on evidence that funding partnerships in support of *certain kinds* of educational change works better than other strategies and thus is worth a major investment.

Let me be more specific. A major goal for the Ford Foundation has been, for many years, to support efforts to expand access to educational opportunities for disadvantaged students. Through the years, we have done a number of things to help students from disadvantaged backgrounds, both in urban and rural settings, more successfully than in the past move through the full K–16 education system. That has been a major focus for the foundation for three decades. We have tried a variety of approaches over that time and have come to feel that a key element is to help various parts or sectors of the educational system fit together more tightly.

Most of the work, though, tended to be sector specific—middle school projects—or activities designed to improve the connection between two parts of the educational pipeline—two- and four-year colleges, for example. But the numbers didn't change that much, except, perhaps, the high school graduation rates for certain population cohorts. College-going rates, the transfer rates from two-year to four-year colleges, baccalaureate attainment rates have not changed much during the last decade for at-risk students. And some would argue that for certain significant parts of the population—Hispanic students, for example—things have actually gotten worse. So, what to do?

This led us to feel that we needed to invest in fully cross-sector work. In work that was truly more K through 16. We needed to work simultaneously with all the parts of the educational system to plug the leaks in the educational pipeline. This led us to feel, minimally, that we needed to foster work through our grants that would help people work collaboratively at the elementary, middle, high school, community college, and senior college levels.

This, though, is just one layer of the collaborative work we are funding—partnerships among K–16 educators. Though working this way seems commonsensical, I still acknowledge that since there are few sustained successful examples of collaborative work of this kind, the jury is still out in regard to whether or not cross-sector collaboration in fact can push the numbers.

More complex, and even more untested, is the attempt to make the collaboration horizontal as well as vertical. If the vertical collaboration represents the K–16 pipeline, the horizontal nature of the work we've been funding now extends to players beyond the schools. The hypothesis here is that schools cannot achieve these ambitious goals on their own. They need the help of community-based groups, corporations, public officials, and the wider public.

Thus it became clear to us that it was worth testing the value of a horizontal collaboration that brings employer groups and parents, community groups, and civic leaders into partnership with the schools. This seems additionally important since we hope the gains that may occur will be sustained; and it is therefore necessary to have at the table, playing critical roles, people who have the ability to shape policy in support of systemic change—representatives from all communities and interested parties.

We are testing the logic that working in this vertically and horizontally integrated way can help contribute to the kinds of improvements and enhanced opportunities that we have been seeking as a foundation for decades.

DM: You are providing a sense of the history of the foundation's three decades of trying to improve access with sector-specific programs and strategies. Is a recognition of the complexity of the levels of education and the many stakeholders vital to students' success driving you toward funding collaborations?

LSZ: It's even more complex than that. In our earlier sector-specific work, we failed to aggregate our work adequately.

For example, take our work to help community colleges enhance their transfer functions. We saw it as important to work on creating curricular pathways so that students moving from community colleges to the four-year colleges would have a coherent math experience or a coherent experience in writing. But nowhere did we attempt to put all the curricular pieces together so that students would have a comprehensive and coherent academic experience. We tended to slice up our work into discrete and separate projects.

In the current iteration of things, we are not only attempting to work across the sectors but we are also attempting to work comprehensively in an integrated and collaborative way *within* the sectors.

DM: You seem to be suggesting a new logic of funding, rooted in a reflection on the limitations of earlier programs. Could you discuss the role of community colleges in collaborations to promote educational access?

LSZ: Let me start with a quick piece of history. One of the Ford Foundation's early initiatives, the Urban Community College Transfer Opportunity Program, during the 1980s, focused on the connection between community colleges and senior institutions. The goal was to see more minority students than in the past earn baccalaureate degrees. We worked with many institutions, a few dozen, over an extended period of time and in truth didn't see much change in their transfer rates. In thinking about what to do next, in response to these disappointing data, we began to feel that it was essential to build stronger connections between high schools and community colleges. We began to fund initiatives such as the Middle College High School, which is an institution that bridges high school and community college by allowing students to enroll simultaneously in both places. This was one of a number of concurrent enrollment strategies we funded that also included, at the other end, projects that allowed enrollment at two- and four-year colleges.

We came to feel that we needed to work with the entire system, to plug the leaks that existed at each transition point. We also wanted to strengthen the quality of education that the students got earlier on, so that by the time they got to community college, and then transferred, they were prepared to succeed. So, the more that we thought about the need to work across the entire K–16 spectrum, the more community colleges began to loom as that nexus institution, an ideally situated bridge between the precollegiate and baccalaureate worlds. And for that reason—they are well positioned to play a connective bridging role—community colleges are more comfortable than senior colleges in working with high schools, while at the same time more comfortable working with senior colleges than are the high schools. They are really of both worlds: the worlds of precollegiate and collegiate education.

Thus the community college emerged for us as the institution that could best help catalyze activity at both ends of the educational spectrum in support of enhanced educational opportunities for disadvantaged students. Therefore, in the successor program to the Urban Community College Transfer Opportunity Program, the Urban Partnership Program, the majority of grantees in the sixteen cities where this work is underway are community colleges.

DM: What characterizes community colleges that are most effective at facilitating collaboration?

LSZ: I would include a presidential leadership that sincerely believes in working in partnership with other institutions. I would look for a track record by the president of having close professional relationships with his or her CEO colleagues, particularly the presidents of the four-year colleges that the community college students go to once they transfer.

Equally important is that the president have strong working relationships with the school superintendent. Obviously it's a bonus if you find that there are strong ties to the business community and to political leadership and community-based organizations. Those are rarer things to find, but if you have any evidence of that at all, that certainly is a signal that a legitimate collaborative brokered by the community college can come into existence.

Another thing that we have found provides evidence that the community college is well suited to play this role is evidence of structural relationships that cross different sectors of the educational system. Most significant are strong, direct partnerships with feeder high schools and the four-year receiving institutions. I would look at the programmatic or discipline level to see whether or not there are examples of math teachers in the high schools and community colleges and four-year colleges somehow being aware of each other and working together, even in casual ways.

DM: Finally, let's discuss the challenge that collaboration poses to the funder. How does it change the ways in which funders think and do business?

LSZ: In an earlier model of philanthropy, a funder would establish priorities to guide grantmaking, set aside resources, convene an advisory group to help develop a fairly prescriptive RFP, and then send it out, announcing a competition. There was not a lot of negotiation between funder and grantee in regard to the overall goals of the initiative, how progress would be measured, or how one would communicate what was learned. There also tended to be little effort to foster learning among grantees. In effect it was a very funder-centered process. In my view this top-down approach is not appropriate when asking groups to collaborate. The funder also needs to be willing to get into the mix.

In addition, in these kinds of collaborative situations, one of the major goals is learning. We need to bring about change and share that learning as widely as possible so that what is gained can be sustained after the external funding ends.

Also, since it's obvious that the people on the ground are going to be the ones that carry out the work and take most of the risks, it seems essential for them to be a part of the process from the very beginning, even from when the goals for the initiative are developed.

This new funding model is an ongoing, dynamic partnership that calls for the people receiving grants *and* the funders to be connected and continuously learning from each other.

L. STEVEN ZWERLING *is senior director, Education, Media, Arts and Culture Program, the Ford Foundation.*

The assessment of collaborative efforts is a complex but vital effort.
Lessons are derived from an assessment of multisite, multi-institutional
collaboratives.

No Pain, No Gain: The Learning Curve in Assessing Collaboratives

Laura I. Rendón, Wendy L. Gans, Mistalene D. Calleroz

The assessment of multisite, multi-institutional K–16 educational collaboratives is a significantly complex challenge. Not only must attention be given to the diversity of locations and institutions but evaluators must also consider issues such as the heterogeneity of social and educational programs; differences in the ways data are accessed, collected, and reported; differences in what program funders expect in the way of assessment; and what grant or contract recipients expect to accomplish and are able and willing to deliver. The challenge becomes even more complex insofar as evaluation is usually viewed with suspicion and fear; further, internal and external political tensions and problems are difficult to bring to the surface with sufficiently exact clarity to find resolution.

Ford Foundation Urban Partnership Program

This chapter presents a case study of an assessment project designed to evaluate the Ford Foundation's Urban Partnership Program (UPP). The UPP is one of the nation's most important initiatives, designed to assist sixteen of the largest U.S. cities to eradicate the barriers that preclude the educational progress of at-risk students. To address this goal, cities developed partnerships—collaborative relationships with key entities such as K–12 schools, two- and four-year colleges and universities, community-based organizations, elected officials, and business and industrial organizations. These partners have a stake in ensuring that all students, regardless of background, had the opportunity to learn and develop their full potential. Collectively, these partnerships have become a voice for at-risk students.

NEW DIRECTIONS FOR COMMUNITY COLLEGES, no. 103, Fall 1998 © Jossey-Bass Publishers

The participating cities in the UPP are Bronx, Chicago, Denver, Houston, Los Angeles, Memphis, Miami, Minneapolis, Newark, Phoenix, Queens, Richmond, Rochester, San Juan (Puerto Rico), Santa Ana, and Seattle. These sixteen cities tested the notion that it takes a partnership to marshal and link community services in order to restructure and integrate the entire K–16 educational pathway. A key element in the success of each partnership has been involving leaders from different sectors, who can use their personal and institutional power to come together and find solutions to shared problems. Citywide alliances have also worked together to share services and resources, develop goals, solve organizational dilemmas, and understand and resolve personal differences. They sought to overcome entrenched layers of damaging attitudes, policies, and practices that worked against student success. UPP collaboratives strived to develop creative solutions, recognizing that there were multiple ways to change social services and educational systems.

UPP Assessment Model

The UPP was initiated in 1991 with a focus on assisting cities to develop initiatives that would break down the barriers to academic success of at-risk students. Providing program leadership and technical assistance was the National Center for Urban Partnerships (NCUP), based at Bronx Community College of the City University of New York. The one nonnegotiable item related to participating in the UPP was that each city must engage in assessment. Partnerships were assured that evaluation results would not be used to withdraw funding and that in fact, assessment was a necessary process for improvement and modification. Subsequently the UPP National Assessment Center was established at Arizona State University to assist collaboratives with designing, collecting, analyzing, and interpreting citywide data, with particular attention paid to the academic progress and outcomes of at-risk students.

The UPP assessment model was conceived in 1992 when the Ford Foundation program officer convened a diverse group of educators, researchers, journalists, and NCUP staff to develop the organizational framework that would guide assessment. At that time it was decided that evaluation would be multimethod (quantitative and qualitative). The focus was to build the capacity for partnerships to conduct their own assessments, so that when Ford Foundation involvement ended, the cities would have a well-designed, field-tested model that they could employ. Other elements included making the model

Easy to understand and implement

Fully participatory, with all collaboratives playing a role in defining the outcomes to be assessed, the data elements to be gathered, and the methodological approach to be followed

Nonthreatening and nonjudgmental

Sufficiently rigorous to ensure worth and credibility

The UPP assessment efforts were to have a national staff, including a director, assessment facilitators who would be assigned to help build capacity in each city, assessment coordinators, who would be contact persons responsible for assessment in each city, and research consultants, who would have expertise in quantitative and qualitative methods.

The goals of the UPP assessment were as follows:

1. To build and strengthen the capacity of each citywide partnership to collect, analyze, interpret, and apply evaluative data in order to bring about systemwide K–16 changes
2. To assist citywide partnerships in conducting a rigorous, high-quality evaluation, resulting in data to help
   a. Ascertain student outcomes and also the factors that may have led to those outcomes
   b. Document strategies that work and factors that might be attributed to students' success or failure
   c. Define the factors that influence the organizational effectiveness of the partnership
3. To employ citywide data from the sixteen partnerships to learn more about what can be done to create systemic change and help collaboratives function more effectively
4. To disseminate research findings in journals, at national conferences, and through other means

In 1996, the Ford Foundation supported a new, primarily qualitative assessment component for determining the extent to which the teams were promoting systemic change. This initiative was a seen as a complement to the ongoing assessment efforts and was located at LaSalle University. Its focus was to learn more about the following issues:

The context of reform efforts at the institutional, city, and state levels
The way the partnership defined and understood systemic change
The history and development of the partnership
The lessons learned by the partnership in the design and implementation of a model of collaboration
The role of interventions and major activities in the partnership
The effect on the partnership of participating in a national consortium

Assessment Theory

It was necessary to employ a theory that was applicable to the UPP as a large-scale, multi-institutional, and complex social program, and this led to the question of which theory to employ. On the one hand there was concern that the assessment clients (Ford Foundation trustees, public policy makers, and so on) would want empirical evidence based on quantitative methods. Moreover, because the desired academic outcome was the baccalaureate degree, it was determined that student academic progress would be tracked through the examination of key quantitative indicators across the K–16 system (that is, high school GPAs, two- to four-year college transfer rates, baccalaureate attainment rates, and so on). On the other hand some of the city stakeholders argued for a constructivist approach based on qualitative methods such as in-person interviews, ethnographies, case studies, and focus groups. These stakeholders believed qualitative methods would tell more about partnership milestones, lessons learned, and systemic change. However, the drawback was that exclusive use of qualitative methods would restrict evaluators mainly to critical contemplation of the program, storytelling, and dialogue with stakeholders.

Consequently, the theory guiding UPP assessment had to represent multiple methods and approaches. Integrating quantitative and qualitative methods is now an accepted evaluation practice, given that both methods are still too much in development to be accorded exclusive status and that the best examples seem to be mixed models (Reichardt and Rallis, 1994). This is not surprising given that evaluations are conducted under many constraints (Datta, 1994) such as short time frames, relatively little money, intractable measurement challenges, scanty baseline information, widely varying agendas, delays in obtaining clearances to access data and in securing additional funding, and the need to minimize demands on others.

It was modern evaluation theorists such as Lee J. Cronbach and Peter H. Rossi who offered a theoretical model that was applicable to the UPP. Cronbach and Rossi are integrators who surveyed diverse theories that have appeared since the 1960s and tried to fit these pieces of a puzzle into a coherent whole. Theirs are contingency theories, which attempt to specify under which circumstances and for which purposes different practices make sense. According to Shadish, Cook, and Leviton (1991), good evaluation practice for social programming is based on five components: theory of social programming, theory of use, theory of knowledge construction, theory of valuing, and theory of evaluation practice. They categorize Cronbach and Rossi as "third-stage" theorists who have, as their major focus, the synthesis of work from preceding stages. Shadish, Cook, and Leviton summarize the theoretical position of Cronbach and Rossi in each of these five components.

In considering the first of the five components, *theory of social programming,* third-stage theorists agree that social programs are politically affected, that they change gradually, that improving existing programs offers the best chance to contribute to short-term social change, and that radical change requires a longer-term perspective. For the second component, *theory of use,* Cronbach and Rossi note the importance of using evaluation to think about issues, define problems, and gain new ideas and perspectives (enlightenment). The theorists also stress that evaluation findings can be used to implement policy (instrumental use).

The third component, *theory of knowledge construction,* is based on the notion that assessment has a place for all methods—case studies, sample surveys, randomized experiments, and so forth. Method choice depends on the strengths and weaknesses of methods for meeting information needs. The fourth component, *theory of valuing,* allows sensitivity to the values of the stakeholders and of the policy-shaping community that evaluators serve.

For the fifth component, *theory of evaluation practice,* both Cronbach and Rossi recommend program monitoring. The goal is to identify implementation problems, ensure the program is designed to meet relevant needs, and discover unexpected outcomes.

Assessment Stages

The first six years of UPP assessment offer a fascinating account of the complexities involved in designing, implementing, correcting, normalizing, and institutionalizing a large-scale evaluation model. The first two years may be viewed as a formative stage, characterized by planning, organizing, building capacity, and gathering data. The second two years may be described as normative, a period of learning, correcting mistakes, and building consensus and support for assessment. The fifth and sixth years were a time of assessment institutionalization. A solid basis for continuing the assessment process was established, with data collection and integration providing tangible results.

Years 1 and 2: UPP Formative Assessment Stage. Year 1 (September 1, 1992, to August 31, 1993) was spent developing the UPP assessment model, staffing, organizing for assessment, and helping collaboratives build the capacity to design and conduct their own assessments. During the formation of the project, it was decided to have yearly assessment meetings that would bring all partnerships together to work on assessment issues. At the first meeting the partnerships decided that assessment would focus on three areas: tracking indicators of student progress across the K–16 system, ascertaining the effectiveness of interventions developed in each city, and determining how well each partnership functioned and operated and the extent to which it was effecting systemic change. Although partnerships were supportive of their new evaluation role, there was some confusion about evaluation expectations and focus and about the use of evaluation.

To clarify these issues, the Ford Foundation program officer took an active role in shaping the assessment effort and communicated three reasons why participating UPP cities were being required to engage in evaluation. First, partnerships were told that it was very unusual for the foundation to make a ten-year commitment to a project. Given the extensive amount of work to be done and the significant foundation commitment, it was to be expected that the foundation would want to know what it was getting for its investment. Second, partnerships were encouraged to be more reflective, sensing, and self-correcting practitioners. Third, partnerships were informed that they had a responsibility to the field of education itself to provide credible data in support of their claims of effectiveness. It was for this last reason that the program officer suggested perhaps the term *assessment* was more appropriate than the term *evaluation*. The former suggests sitting together in a collaborative fashion to engage in the process of discovery of meaning in the work of the partnerships. Assessment thus became the operable term defining the work of the UPP—a work in progress, an investigative process that was exploratory rather than confirmatory and judgmental.

To provide focus and direction at the local level during Year 1, partnerships were asked to develop evaluation plans that specified objectives, the areas to be assessed, timelines, methods to be used to assess each area, and evaluation questions to be addressed. These plans would serve as the blueprints for conducting assessment in each of the cities. The plans were reviewed by the national assessment staff and suggestions were made for improvement. Cities that had strong connections with local evaluation experts or teams including such experts tended to have the best plans.

In Year 2 (September 1, 1993, to August 31, 1994), work began on collecting numerical data on indicators of student progress and the effectiveness of the partnerships. These quantitative data were viewed as baseline information that would give collaboratives a better sense of where problems with student progress existed, in order that corrective strategies could be implemented. Because partnerships asked for more direction and specificity in their assessment efforts, assessment staff and city stakeholders collaborated to produce the *Evaluation Manual* (Rendón, Nora, and London, 1994), which was then sent to each city.

The manual included sections on setting objectives for each educational tier and on matching objectives with activities. It also contained twenty-two tables for which partnerships were to provide student progress data. In addition, the manual included the Student Aspirations Survey, which was to be administered to a random sample of students at the sixth, eighth, tenth, and twelfth grade levels. It also contained a survey designed to assess the citywide partnership, which was to be administered to key alliance leaders and returned to the assessment director.

Years 1 and 2: Lessons Learned. Years 1 and 2 offered several valuable lessons about organizing a large-scale assessment project:

Organizing for assessment in a large-scale program takes time and patience. Careful attention must be given to staffing, responding to local needs, clarifying purpose, setting clear goals, and alleviating apprehensions among all parties involved about the use of assessment data.

The involvement of the program officer in stressing the importance and role of assessment is critical throughout the course of the program.

The best evaluation plans are those that are crafted with an assessment team or local evaluation experts.

Despite funding agency efforts to grant autonomy in planning and conducting assessment, stakeholders are likely to seek direction about what the agency "really" wants. Consequently, assessment staff has to continually involve stakeholders in evaluation planning and in the crafting of documents that will be locally employed.

Years 3 and 4: UPP Normative Assessment Stage. Throughout Year 3 (September 1, 1994, to August 31, 1995), the collaboratives were intensely involved in assessment—tracking indicators of student progress, assessing their interventions, and examining the functioning and operability of the partnership itself. They were also beginning to note their achievements, challenges, and problems with assessment.

Year 3: Achievements, Challenges, and Problems. City assessment coordinators reported how assessment had been useful in their partnerships in the following areas:

Employment of evaluation plans. The assessment process provided collaboratives the opportunity to conceptualize and design their own evaluation plans that served as blueprints to conduct assessment.

Integration of assessment into the work of the partnership. Cities were beginning to see the importance of engaging in assessment; assessment led to instituting permanent evaluation groups and creating, updating, and expanding demographic databases.

Increased collaboration with key stakeholders. For many coordinators, the assessment process was key in establishing or consolidating working relationships among the partnership's constituencies.

Advancement of fundraising. Several coordinators established a direct link between fundraising and the assessment process.

Despite important positive benefits of evaluation, the assessment project also faced numerous challenges and problems, some of which are commonly associated with assessment efforts. City assessment coordinators reported on the following issues:

Trust. Often, evaluation bears a negative stigma, and suspicion arose about the "real" intent of the evaluation. Concerns were expressed that evaluation would be used as a tool to withdraw funds from the program and that it was a mechanism to generate more work for everyone involved in the project. The assessment director and program officer had to emphasize that funds would not be withdrawn as a result of "negative" data findings.

Direction and autonomy. From the very beginning, the assessment staff had to walk a fine line between being prescriptive and allowing collaboratives the autonomy to "do their own thing." Tensions occurred when some partnerships felt there was a specific evaluation format or plan that the foundation wanted the cities to follow. At the same time, the partnerships were being told that this was not a top-down evaluation and that they should be taking the necessary steps to develop their own assessment plans.

Ability to track students over time. Initially it was thought that partnerships would be able to track students over a period of time. However, logistical considerations led to the realization that at least during the beginning years, the partnerships would have to conduct a trend analysis of students, as opposed to a causal longitudinal study. There were numerous barriers to the latter study: some partnerships had no interventions in a particular tier; the interventions varied among cities, not only in their type but in their location (that is, elementary, middle, and high schools; two- and four-year institutions); there was student mobility in an open system; and there was staff turnover. Someone in each city would have to be assigned to follow the cohort and examine data over multiple years, which would involve issues of cost, staff reliability, and time.

The benefit of a trend study was that it provided baseline data on students in all participating institutions during identified years to give cities an idea of how well students were doing and where problems might be occurring. The drawback of a trend study was that the cohort changed yearly and there was no way to draw causal inferences between what the UPP offered and the extent to which students achieved academic progress.

Staff workload. City teams continually pointed out that they were consumed with work and that assessment was taking up much of their time. Most of the city assessment coordinators were involved only part-time and had to recruit others to help. They stressed the need for more staff or consultants. In addition, some coordinators felt they did not have the academic training to do assessment. And some said local politics were a factor in evaluation (that is, there were issues of access to and ownership of data) that often took time and effort to negotiate.

Lack of funding. Collaboratives continually expressed their need for additional funding to deal with assessment. They cited their need of support for personnel costs and statistical analysis expenses (that is, computer time, paper, postage, report production).

Role of the assessment facilitator. Assessment facilitators or consultants, who felt that their role was to provide technical assistance on assessment, found that when they made city site visits, they were often asked for assistance in developing proposals and interventions.

Staff turnover. Several city assessment coordinators left their positions. Their replacements had to be quick studies to engage in assessment.

Collaboration between city directors and assessment coordinators. How the assessment coordinator and the partnership director could collaborate on evaluation and who should initiate that collaboration was not clear to the participants.

Connection of assessment to programming. It was a challenge to avoid making assessment an add-on activity and to integrate assessment with the UPP's programming efforts.

Evaluation manual problems. The *Evaluation Manual* proved to be generally unworkable. Problems included difficulties in generating uniform data across cities, lack of timely reporting, data sensitivity, data unavailability, and differing levels of partnership readiness to engage in assessment.

UPP National Assessment Center team mistakes. First, the assessment team erroneously assumed that the *Evaluation Manual* would work by and large because the partnerships had been involved in its creation. In fact the manual should have been field-tested more thoroughly to ensure its workability. Second, the team assumed that the partnerships were convinced that they should be tracking quantitative indicators of student progress. However, some cities felt there should be less emphasis on quantitative findings and more on a qualitative approach to capturing lessons learned. Third, because of the problems with the *Evaluation Manual,* some collaboratives felt reinforced in their belief that this type of national data collection was unlikely to work.

At one level, such problems and errors could be considered a setback to the total assessment effort. To be sure, tensions mounted, and some partnerships were apprehensive about what would happen next. However, several collaboratives did understand the nature of assessment and that often it takes trial and error to get a complicated process on the right track. At another level, these mistakes and their consequences provided an important opportunity to reshape the assessment effort. Rather than bemoan the mistakes, the national assessment team, in conjunction with the program officer and NCUP staff, set about to make some significant midcourse corrections that involved city stakeholders.

Year 4: Recalibration. During Year 4 (September 1, 1995, to July 31, 1996) a great deal of time was spent on recalibrating the assessment process. The assessment director contacted several city directors and coordinators to get their sense of what the problems were and how they might be resolved. In addition, the program officer and the assessment director hosted an assessment study group meeting in New York at the Ford Foundation. This meeting was quite productive in that city leaders were given an opportunity to work together with foundation representatives and NCUP staff to solve the most pressing assessment problems. For example, partnerships urged that the number of quantitative indicators of student progress be scaled down to only those that were absolutely essential. They also argued successfully that the foundation fund the assessment of systemic change taking place in their cities. And they wanted to be sure that qualitative data such as lessons learned, milestones, and student success stories would be captured in a systematic fashion. It should be noted that the program officer's involvement was absolutely critical to the recalibration of the assessment process, for his leadership was viewed as a positive sign that continual negotiations with stakeholders would assure that assessment was based on city needs and realities.

The essence of this initial study group meeting was continued at the fourth assessment meeting, held in Los Angeles, December 1995. At this meeting, participants reduced the number of quantitative tables from twenty-two to nine. The program officer and NCUP staff made additional suggestions to improve the assessment framework. City leaders also became more invested in assessment; they now believed the foundation and the national assessment staff were listening to their concerns and actually doing something about them. The program officer planned a second assessment study group in January 1996 for a group of self-described "renegades" who, despite acknowledging the efforts to improve the process, still expressed reservations about it. Through open discussions this meeting alleviated the renegades' apprehensions, and they too became enthusiastic about assessment. All of these discussions and negotiations led to the development of the *Assessment Guide* (Rendón, Nora, and London, 1996), a new effort designed to replace the old *Evaluation Manual*.

Completed in Year 4, the final version of the *Assessment Guide* focused on these three assessment areas:

Quantitative indicators of student progress. The nine tables included in the *Assessment Guide* were designed to show persistence rates from the end of elementary school to the beginning of middle school, persistence rates from the end of middle school to the beginning of high school, high school graduation rates, mean high school GPA, college-going rates, first- to second-year college reenrollment rates, transfer rates from two- to four-year institutions, associate degrees earned, and baccalaureate degrees earned by native and transfer students.

Intervention indicators. Partnerships were to submit a report that assessed at least one intervention on a yearly basis. The assessment could be quantitative, qualitative, or both.

Systemic change indicators. Collaboratives were to work with a coordinator of qualitative assessment, who was to assign a local "insider/outsider" to work with each city. This person, who might be familiar with the city but would not be someone who worked with the partnership, was to collect qualitative data that captured the different ways partnerships were affecting systemic change throughout the K–16 system.

The *Assessment Guide* also included the UPP Five-Year Assessment Framework. It specified the relationships among the three assessment areas, how they might influence student achievement, and how data from the three areas would be integrated.

In summary, Year 4 proved to be a most productive time for UPP assessment. Tensions were alleviated, enthusiasm for assessment was restored, and complaints diminished. Assessment was put on the right track, a formidable achievement for a complex, large-scale assessment effort such as that required by the UPP.

Years 3 and 4: Lessons Learned. Many assessment efforts go by the wayside when conflicts arise. This was not true in the UPP. Although the makings of an assessment effort gone awry were certainly present, neither the program officer, the assessment staff, nor the partnerships allowed conflicts to remain unresolved. The lessons learned include the following:

The assessment function of a project should be conceptualized and implemented as soon as the program is created. Otherwise, it can carry the stigma of an add-on activity.

Evaluation can be viewed more positively if it is described as assessment—a learning process involving multiple stakeholders, designed to improve, not to judge.

Designing a data collection manual or guide to be used by a number of different partnerships is a sensitive, complex, and difficult task that involves continual dialogue with stakeholders, field-testing, revisions, and patience.

Without continual exchange and review of ideas, stakeholders are likely to believe that their needs are not being considered and that assessment is really a top-down effort.

Individuals in charge of large-scale assessment projects are more effective when they possess both basic knowledge about evaluation theory and practice *and* such personal qualities as tolerance for ambiguity, patience, good listening skills, willingness to collaborate, a sense of humor, and openness to change.

The good news about a large-scale assessment effort is that despite its sensitive and complex nature, it can be designed and implemented to reflect multiple local needs and to gain the support and endorsement of all collaboratives.

Years 5 and 6: UPP Assessment Institutionalization Stage. By Year 5 (August 1, 1996, to July 31, 1997) and into Year 6, assessment efforts had developed to the point that successful activities occurred in many areas as assessment became institutionalized in the work of the partnerships. This stage was marked by these outcomes:

Collaboration and cooperation. During this time city directors and assessment coordinators were often in touch with UPP National Assessment Center staff at Arizona State University, asking questions and providing input for items under review. Indeed, at NCUP meetings during these years, comments from city directors and assessment coordinators about assessment were generally very positive. One representative remarked, "In our city, assessment is our friend." Statements about the now collaborative nature of the process were common. Partnership leaders especially appreciated open lines of communication, continual feedback, detailed explanations about use of data, assistance with understanding the overall problems in data collection, and local understanding and ownership of assessment. In addition, several who were once renegades made public remarks at the national conference on how very far the process had come in the past four years.

Generation of useful quantitative data and revisions to the process. Most partnerships were able to submit quantitative data for the nine tables in the *Assessment Guide*. These data tables were analyzed by the UPP assessment team, and a report of the findings (Rendón, Nora, Gans, and Calleroz, 1997b) was prepared and presented to city directors and assessment coordinators at the annual NCUP conference in October 1997. Participants engaged in a dialogue about policies and practices in relation to the data and shared data that reflected student outcomes.

Ongoing meetings among the program officer, NCUP and assessment staff, and city leaders led to the recommendation to collect standardized test score information. Test score data were viewed as essential determinants of college eligibility for at-risk students. Consequently five new tables were added to the revised *Assessment Guide* (Rendón, Nora, Gans, and Calleroz, 1997a). They covered elementary school achievement test scores, middle school achievement test scores, high school achievement test scores, mean scores on the SAT, and mean scores on the ACT. Partnerships also developed and submitted their intervention assessment plans and reports.

Generation of reports focusing on systemic change. Several partnerships, in conjunction with the coordinator of qualitative assessment, produced detailed reports on systemic change, which were widely disseminated. Plans were made to integrate the data findings from the quantitative indicators of student progress, the intervention indicators, and the systemic change indicators. This important task represents the next significant challenge in UPP assessment.

Quantification of student success. Partnerships were able to quantify the success they were having with students in partnership interventions. Some examples of their "victories with students" are improved scores on standardized state basic skills tests at the elementary, middle, and high school levels; instances of schools removed from probationary status; and improved transfer and persistence rates.

Significant decline of criticism. The smoothest running years in the UPP assessment were Years 5 and 6. Tensions were eased, complaints diminished, and trust developed between the assessment team and city representatives.

Conclusion

This UPP assessment case study reveals how an unconventional evaluation effort for collaboratives overcame typical problems and moved toward normalization and institutionalization. The UPP assessment process took leadership, hard work, countless negotiations, patience, and recalibration. This development process was somewhat predictable, as it progressed from formative to normative and on to an institutionalization stage. Pain led to gain. As the UPP assessment moves forward to the year 2000, the project continues to gain purpose from being a shared learning experience.

References

Datta, L. "Paradigm Wars: A Basis for Peaceful Coexistence and Beyond." In C. S. Reichardt and S. F. Rallis (eds.), *The Qualitative-Quantitative Debate: New Perspectives.* New Directions for Program Evaluation, no. 61. San Francisco: Jossey-Bass, 1994.

Reichardt, C. S., and Rallis, S. F. "Qualitative and Quantitative Inquiries Are Not Incompatible: A Call for a New Partnership." In C. S. Reichardt and S. F. Rallis (eds.), *The Qualitative-Quantitative Debate: New Perspectives.* New Directions for Program Evaluation, no. 61. San Francisco: Jossey-Bass, 1994.

Rendón, L. I., Nora, A., Gans, W. L., and Calleroz, M. D. *Assessment Guide: Second Reporting Year.* Tempe: Arizona State University, 1997a.

Rendón, L. I., Nora, A., Gans, W. L., and Calleroz, M. D. *Student Academic Progress: Key Data Trends, Baseline 1995–96.* Tempe: Arizona State University, 1997b.

Rendón, L. I., Nora, A., and London, H. *Evaluation Manual.* Tempe: Arizona State University, 1994.

Rendón, L. I., Nora, A., and London, H. *Assessment Guide.* Tempe: Arizona State University, 1996.

Shadish, W. R., Cook, D. T., and Leviton, L. C. *Foundations of Program Evaluation.* Thousand Oaks, Calif.: Sage, 1991.

LAURA I. RENDÓN is professor of educational leadership at Arizona State University and director of assessment for the Ford Foundation Urban Partnership Program.

WENDY L. GANS is program coordinator at the Assessment Center, Ford Foundation Urban Partnership Program, Arizona State University.

MISTALENE D. CALLEROZ is a research assistant at the Assessment Center, Ford Foundation Urban Partnership Program, Arizona State University.

This chapter outlines the resources that can fuel collaborative relationships, including funding sources and examples of successful partnerships.

Sources and Information: Community Colleges and Collaboration

Erika Yamasaki

The following ERIC publications discuss the scope of collaborative activities undertaken by community colleges and their diverse partners, the types of agencies that fund such programs, and the strategies that guide effective partnerships. As a result of collaborative relationships, satellite campuses and high school partnerships have been established, transfer rates have increased, and concerns such as child care have been addressed. Funding sources for all the different programs vary from foundations and national retail chains to local businesses, cities, and the colleges themselves. The resource publications described here include reports on several regional, statewide, and local efforts and also information on the need for collaboration, the benefits of collaboration, and guidelines for collaborative success. These resources may prove helpful to institutions interested in forming their own collaborative relationships.

Most ERIC documents (publications with ED numbers) can be viewed on microfiche at over nine hundred libraries worldwide. In addition, most may be ordered on microfiche or on paper from the ERIC Document Reproduction Services (EDRS) by calling (800) 443-ERIC. Journal articles are not available from EDRS, but they can be acquired through regular library channels or purchased from one of the following article reproduction services: Carl Uncover, Internet: http://www.carl.org/uncover/, E-mail: uncover@carl.org, telephone: (800) 787-7979; UMI, E-mail: orders@infostore.com, telephone: (800) 248-0360; and ISI, E-mail: tga@isinet.com, telephone:(800) 523-1850.

Existing Partnerships

These documents illustrate the range of activities in which community colleges engage through collaborative relationships with businesses, cities, other institutions of higher education, and various public agencies.

Clark, L. M., and Tullar, P. "Three Governmental Entities Collaborate to Build a Satellite Community College Campus in Northern Arizona: Working Together to Create a 'One-Stop Learning Center.'" Flagstaff, Ariz.: Coconino Community College, 1995. (ED 395 618)

In an effort to develop a "one-stop learning center" to provide educational and library services to a remote community in northern Arizona, Coconino Community College (CCC), Northern Arizona University (NAU), and the city of Page collaborated to create a CCC satellite campus in Page. The new facility will allow CCC to serve more than six hundred students, provide more classes, and expand student services in a cost-effective manner to meet growing demand. In the cooperative effort, the city donated approximately twenty-five acres of land for the project; CCC will construct the library building, equip the library, and supplement the city library's acquisitions efforts and services; and NAU will install the computerized library database. The instructional space of the facility will consist of traditional and interactive instructional television classrooms, vocational and technical laboratories, an art laboratory, a large multipurpose lecture classroom, and science and computer laboratories. The student support services will include a learning enhancement center, an English as a Second Language lab, and a student lounge area.

Marciniak, M. P. "Establishing a Major Off-Campus Center: The Midlands Model." University Center, Mich.: Delta College, 1995. (ED 411 921)

Delta College, a community college in Michigan, used a vacant high school in Midland County as an off-campus, community-based facility. With limited resources the college transformed the school into an instructional site to serve students in their communities, enhance college visibility, and serve increasing enrollment. To accomplish these goals, several steps were required, including collaborating with community leaders and conducting needs assessments; developing a handbook for faculty teaching at the center; staffing beyond job descriptions; contracting services; acquiring furnishings; and enhancing student services, technology, learning services, and collegiality. The purposes and functions of the Delta College center are to provide community residents with access to educational services, a unique learning environment tailored to the community's needs, programs that develop creativity as well as provide career training, a high-quality teaching and learning environment, and formal and informal experiences promoting the social and cultural diversity of the community.

Schlack, M. "The Arcadia Commons Partnership: The Community College and Economic Redevelopment." Kalamazoo, Mich.: Kalamazoo Valley Community College, 1993. (ED 358 887)

Arcadia Commons (AC) in Kalamazoo, Michigan, is a business education park developed through the combined efforts of the Kalamazoo Valley Community College (KVCC), area business and financial institutions, and the Kalamazoo Public Museum. Together they formed the partnership Downtown

Kalamazoo Incorporated (DKI). KVCC's involvement resulted from its need to find new space for its downtown satellite campus, which offers basic skills, employee training, and retraining courses. AC project funding came from DKI members, a federal grant, and a special city business tax. Among the AC projects and partners are a five-star hotel refurbished by the Upjohn Company; KVCC's downtown center, which will serve more than five thousand students and complement programs on the main campus; the West Michigan Cancer Center, a joint venture of Kalamazoo's two regional health care providers; and the refurbished offices of the Visiting Nurse Association of Southwest Michigan. The capstone of the AC is the $20 million educational New Museum, under the stewardship of KVCC, with hands-on exhibits exploring the science, culture, and technology of Southwest Michigan.

Brown, J. L. "The High School Partnership at Kansas City Kansas Community College." Kansas City: Kansas City Kansas Community College, 1993. (ED 362 244)
    The Kansas City Kansas Community College (KCKCC) High School Partnership Program was established in spring 1987 to enable outstanding high school seniors to earn both high school and college credit for college-level courses taken on their high school campuses. Through the partnership program, KCKCC offers classes at ten of the seventeen high schools in its service area. When the program was first initiated, 28 students enrolled for 84 credit hours. By spring 1993, 239 students were enrolled for 924 credit hours. The high school faculty that teach in the program are recommended by their districts and approved by KCKCC personnel. They then become part of KCKCC's adjunct faculty and receive the same compensation. The classes, which are offered in response to requests from the school district, are held on the high school campuses during the regular school day. Compared to on-campus KCKCC classes, partnership classes may meet on a different schedule, but their student performance requirements, textbooks, and total class hours each semester are the same. The program has helped KCKCC establish positive connections with many of its feeder high schools and has elevated its image in the larger community.

Funding Sources

These documents describe collaborative programs supported by various types of funders.

Boone, E. J. *The Academy for Community College Leadership Advancement, Innovation, and Modeling (ACCLAIM)*. Raleigh: North Carolina State University, 1992. (ED 340 438)
    The Academy for Community College Leadership, Innovation, and Modeling (ACCLAIM) is a three-year pilot project funded by the W. K. Kellogg Foundation, North Carolina State University, and the community college systems of Maryland, Virginia, South Carolina, and North Carolina. ACCLAIM's

purpose is to help the region's community colleges assume a leadership role in community-based programming and in effecting collaboration among community leaders and organizations in order to identify and seek solutions to critical concerns. The program has four main components: a continuing education program for community college presidents, administrators, faculty, governance officials, and other community leaders; a doctoral degree program in community college leadership; the development and dissemination of resource materials on strategic planning, environmental scanning, mapping community college publics, identifying and involving community leaders, networking, assessing needs, forming coalitions, conducting community development, and evaluating; and collaborative university program enrichment.

Campbell, L., and Dahl, J. *Mervyn's Family-to-Family Initiative in Oregon.* Paper presented at the Family Day Care Technical Assistance Conference, Atlanta, Apr. 1991. (ED 336 185).
      Family-to-Family is a two-year collaboration among community colleges, public agencies, and businesses in Oregon. It is funded by Mervyn's department stores, and its purpose is to enhance the quality of family child care in the state by training care providers, assisting providers to achieve national accreditation, and educating consumers to recognize and demand high-quality child care.

National Center for Academic Achievement and Transfer, and American Council on Education. "Fostering Institutional Change to Strengthen Transfer: Partnership Grants (Phase II) and Core Curriculum Grants. Projects Funded August 1991." *Transfer Working Papers,* 1991, *2* (6), 1–7. (ED 345 808)
      The Partnership Grant Program of the National Center for Academic Achievement and Transfer awards grants to partnerships between two- and four-year institutions to strengthen transfer, especially for low-income African American and Hispanic students. It also awards Core Curriculum Grants to partnerships between two- and four-year institutions that focus exclusively on curriculum development and require the expansion or redesign of curricula across at least two disciplines or in interdisciplinary studies. Focusing on institutional change in teaching and learning practices, the grants support faculty collaboration. Strong administrative support and methods to monitor the effectiveness of transfer are essential components of both grant programs.

Falcone, L. *Building Coalitions for the Fight Against Drugs: Community College Initiatives.* Washington, D.C.: American Association of Community Colleges, 1993. (ED 365 376)
      In an effort to initiate community-based educational efforts for the prevention and treatment of substance abuse, the American Association of Community Colleges and the Metropolitan Life Foundation sponsored the Community College Alcohol and Other Drug Abuse Education/Training Initiative. Fifteen participating institutions were awarded two-year grants of up

to $10,000 to develop and deliver drug abuse education and training programs in partnership with community groups.

Guidelines for Establishing Collaborative Relationships

The following documents describe various approaches to establishing successful collaborative relationships between community colleges and community-based organizations.

Kussrow, P. G. "Why Community Colleges Need Organizational Partnerships." Position paper, Florida Atlantic University, 1995. (ED 386 230)

Kussrow makes the argument that community problems often are so large in scope that community colleges can respond effectively only by forming organizational partnerships. Prior to establishing these relationships, however, there must be a mutual belief in the need for partnership, and communication among all participating agencies. Furthermore, Kussrow advocates the necessity of an understanding of each party's needs and constraints; an understanding of each partner's role; an appreciation of the structure, funding, and size of the other partners; a continued focus on mutual benefits; an awareness of existing commitments; mutually developed goals and measurable objectives; and a periodic evaluation of partnership agreements. As resources and expertise are shared in areas of overlapping services, activities and staff time can be focused to expand each agency's original area of service. Other benefits of partnerships include reduced costs; better use of existing buildings, staff, equipment, and other resources; nonduplication of services; and lower taxes. Examples of partnerships formed and operating in North Carolina under these guidelines include the Catawba Valley Community College horticulture technology program, developed with the aid of local business owners and the Gaston College partnership with local schools, and the Economic Development Commission of Lincoln County to provide technical and vocational lessons for high school students.

To Help High-Risk Students Succeed. Beacon Guide. Salem, Oreg.: Chemeketa Community College, 1992. (ED 346 926)

The goal of the American Association of Community Colleges' Beacon Colleges Initiative is to disseminate information about exemplary collaborative programs and services. In Oregon, Chemeketa Community College is a Beacon College that has been working in association with five other community colleges in the state to build community beyond the campus by collaborating with employers and agencies to help high-risk students succeed. This guide, designed as a resource for those wishing to initiate collaborative projects of their own, presents an overview of efforts undertaken by this Oregon consortium. The guide includes background information on key concepts, services, and issues related to programs for high-risk community college students. It also contains summaries of model projects; descriptions of funding sources; and lists of external partners, major activities, and contact people.

Vaughan, G. B. "Community-Based Programming: The Community College as Leader and Catalyst." Southern Association of Community, Junior, and Technical Colleges Occasional Paper, 1993, *11* (1), 1–4.

Community-based programming (CBP) envisions a cooperative process in which the community college serves as the leader and catalyst in effecting collaboration among members of its community. Such collaboration not only helps bring about community renewal but brings benefits to colleges as well. In this program overview, CBP is noted as an approach that allows a rational process of decision making and helps institutions deal with long-term choices instead of focusing merely on day-to-day problems. CBP also provides an ongoing process for evaluating the college mission, which can often be pulled in many directions and misunderstood by the college community or the community at large. By providing a means for building broad-based support, CBP ensures that there will be more people working to obtain resources for the college and also allows the community to use its resources more effectively and efficiently. Also CBP provides a means for individual as well as community renewal, by placing the responsibility and authority for community renewal with the individual, thereby placing each citizen in charge of his or her own fate. Finally, CBP assists communities to use their resources more effectively by working with other organizations.

Harlacher, E. L., and Gollattscheck, J. F. *The Community-Building College: Leading the Way to Community Revitalization.* Washington, D.C.: American Association of Community Colleges, 1996. (ED 395 607)

Arguing that the nation's educational system must be renewed to empower citizens and communities, this two-part monograph describes the importance of building learning communities and offers a blueprint to guide community colleges in this undertaking. Establishing partnerships with the community and its organizations and developing a community-based curriculum are central to the goal. Together, colleges and their communities can define a common vision of the future and translate that vision into programs and services. This monograph addresses specific issues in the implementation of a community-based curriculum, including the use of a task force and the development of a five-year action plan.

Johnson, L. (ed.). "Common Ground: Exemplary Community College and Corporate Partnerships." Mission Viejo, Calif.: League for Innovation in the Community College, 1996.

This monograph contains descriptions of fourteen exemplary partnerships between community colleges and corporations. Each narrative discusses how a specific partnership was formed; its structure, organization, and funding; and the lessons learned in the process. Among the partnerships featured are Central Piedmont Community College (Virginia) and Okuma America, Delta College (Michigan) and General Motors Corporation, South Seattle Community College (Washington) and the Boeing Company, and St. Louis Community College (Missouri) and McDonnell-Douglas Corporation.

Stevenson, J. M. "Systemic Leadership Strategies for Community Colleges Initiating Partnerships with Corporations and Schools." Paper presented at the Leadership 2000 national conference of the League for Innovation in the Community College, Washington, D.C., July 1993. (ED 361 012)

Methodologies for undertaking "systemic leadership initiatives," that is, approaches to sharing resources based on collaborative networking, are reviewed in this report. Emphasis is placed on intersector partnerships between community colleges, corporations, and secondary schools. Following an overview of existing partnerships and a review of the literature, this report addresses resistance to collaborative partnerships on the part of both educators and industry. Discussions about the systemic leader's role in bridging the gap between institutional resources and corporate and community needs, transitions from traditional management and leadership approaches to systemic initiatives, and autonomy within systemic planning are also included.

Evaluation and Training Institute. "Partnerships with the Public Sector: Vocational Education Resource Package." Los Angeles: Evaluation and Training Institute, 1993. (ED 357 792)

Designed to assist community college administrators and faculty in enhancing vocational education programs and services, this resource package contains information on successful partnership programs involving California Community Colleges (CCC) and public sector entities. Partnerships highlighted in this report include the Career Path Exploration Program at Foothill College, a mentorship program conducted in collaboration with the Women in Business Committee of the Mountain View Chamber of Commerce; the Greater Avenues for Independence Consortium of the West Valley-Mission Community College District, a program assisting public welfare recipients to achieve economic self-sufficiency; the Hispanic Women's Mentorship Program at Cypress College, conducted in collaboration with the Fairview Development Center and using mentors to increase retention of Hispanic women in the psychiatric technician program at the college; and the Southwestern College cooperative education program with the Navy, a partnership that provides students with internships at Navy command posts.

ERIKA YAMASAKI is a doctoral candidate in the Division of Higher Education and Organizational Change, University of California at Los Angeles, and publications assistant for the ERIC Clearinghouse for Community Colleges.

INDEX

Back Issue/Subscription Order Form

Copy or detach and send to:

Jossey-Bass Inc., Publishers, 350 Sansome Street, San Francisco CA 94104-1342

Call or fax toll free!

Phone 888-378-2537 6AM-5PM PST; Fax 800-605-2665

Back issues: Please send me the following issues at $22 each

(Important: please include series initials and issue number, such as CC90)

1. CC _____

_____

_____

$ _____ Total for single issues

$ _____ Shipping charges (for single issues *only;* subscriptions are exempt from shipping charges): Up to $30, add $5^{50} • $30^{01}–$50, add $6^{50} $50^{01}–$75, add $7^{50} • $75^{01}–$100, add $9 • $100^{01}–$150, add $10 Over $150, call for shipping charge

Subscriptions   Please ❑ start ❑ renew my subscription to *New Directions for Community Colleges* for the year 19___ at the following rate:

❑ Individual $57   ❑ Institutional $107

NOTE: Subscriptions are quarterly, and are for the calendar year only. Subscriptions begin with the spring issue of the year indicated above. For shipping outside the U.S., please add $25.

$ _____ Total single issues and subscriptions (CA, IN, NJ, NY and DC residents, add sales tax for single issues. NY and DC residents must include shipping charges when calculating sales tax. NY and Canadian residents only, add sales tax for subscriptions)

❑ Payment enclosed (U.S. check or money order only)

❑ VISA, MC, AmEx, Discover Card #_____ Exp. date_____

Signature _____ Day phone _____

❑ Bill me (U.S. institutional orders only. Purchase order required)

Purchase order #_____

Name _____

Address _____

_____

_____

Phone_____ E-mail _____

For more information about Jossey-Bass Publishers, visit our Web site at:
www.josseybass.com   **PRIORITY CODE = ND1**